基于“深度学习”的小学英语主题听说教学研究课题成果

听说教学资源与课程设计

针对性听说指导　培养听说能力

简臻红　编著

中国文联出版社

图书在版编目（C I P）数据

听说教学资源与课程设计 / 简臻红编著. -- 北京 :
中国文联出版社, 2024.4
ISBN 978-7-5190-5513-4

Ⅰ. ①听… Ⅱ. ①简… Ⅲ. ①英语－听说教学－教学
研究－小学 Ⅳ. ①G623.312

中国国家版本馆 CIP 数据核字(2024)第 090951 号

编　　著　简臻红
责任编辑　付劲草
责任校对　赵计君
装帧设计　王俊梅

出版发行　中国文联出版社有限公司
社　　址　北京市朝阳区农展馆南里 10 号　　邮编　100125
电　　话　010-85923025（发行部）　010-85923091（总编室）
经　　销　全国新华书店等
印　　刷　德富泰（唐山）印务有限公司

开　　本　710 毫米 x 1000 毫米　1/16
印　　张　18.5
字　　数　250 千字
版　　次　2024 年 4 月第 1 版第 1 次印刷
定　　价　56.00 元

目　录

CONTENTS

一年级主题 1　School　001

一年级主题 2　Body Organs　005

一年级主题 3　Animals　008

一年级主题 4　Numbers　012

一年级主题 5　Colors　015

一年级主题 6　Fruits　018

一年级主题 7　Preposition of Place　021

一年级主题 8　Garfield House　026

一年级主题 9　Toys　031

一年级主题 10　Food　033

一年级主题 11　Drink　037

一年级主题 12　Clothes　041

二年级主题 1　My Family　046
二年级主题 2　Boys and Girls　052
二年级主题 3　My Friends　058
二年级主题 4　In the Community　063
二年级主题 5　In the Park　067
二年级主题 6　Happy Holidays　071
二年级主题 7　Playtime　075
二年级主题 8　Weather　079
二年级主题 9　Seasons　082
二年级主题 10　Times　086
二年级主题 11　My Day　090
二年级主题 12　My Week　094

三年级主题 1　Myself　098
三年级主题 2　My Body　102
三年级主题 3　Food　105
三年级主题 4　Pets　109
三年级主题 5　Clothes　112
三年级主题 6　Birthday　115
三年级主题 7　My School Subjects　118
三年级主题 8　My School　124
三年级主题 9　After School Activities　128
三年级主题 10　Hat　133
三年级主题 11　Family Activities　137
三年级主题 12　My Home　142

四年级主题 1 Sports and Games 146
四年级主题 2 On the Weekend 149
四年级主题 3 Transportation 152
四年级主题 4 Asking for Help 155
四年级主题 5 Safety 158
四年级主题 6 Jobs 161
四年级主题 7 My Neighbourhood 164
四年级主题 8 Cities 168
四年级主题 9 Travel Plans 173
四年级主题 10 Hobbies 177
四年级主题 11 Free Time 181
四年级主题 12 Countries 184

五年级主题 1 Classmates 187
五年级主题 2 Teachers 193
五年级主题 3 Animals 197
五年级主题 4 Shopping Day 201
五年级主题 5 TV Shows 206
五年级主题 6 Chores 209
五年级主题 7 Keeping Healthy 212
五年级主题 8 Special Day 217
五年级主题 9 Making Contact 221
五年级主题 10 Have a Great Trip 225
五年级主题 11 Have a Magical Trip 229
五年级主题 12 Growing up 233

六年级主题 1 In China 237

六年级主题 2 Around the World 241

六年级主题 3 Animals 245

六年级主题 4 Feelings 249

六年级主题 5 Famous People 253

六年级主题 6 The Spring Festival 258

六年级主题 7 Visiting Zhuhai 262

六年级主题 8 All Around Me 268

六年级主题 9 Daily Life 271

六年级主题 10 Free Time 275

六年级主题 11 Nature and Culture 279

六年级主题 12 Summer Vacation 282

一年级主题 1 School

听力材料

Part A: – Good morning!

– Good morning!

I want a brush.

– Hello!

– Hello.

– What's your name?

– My name is Ma Liang.

– You are a good boy. I have a magic brush.

– Thank you.

– Goodbye.

– Goodbye.

I have **a magic brush**!

I have **a magic hen**!

– Show me your **ruler**.

– I have **a ruler**.

– Show me your **pencil**.

– I have **a pencil**.

– Show me your **book**.

– I have **a book**.

– Show me your **schoolbag**.

– I have **a schoolbag**.

Part B: – Show me your **gold**.

– I have **some gold**.

– Show me your **ship**.

– I have **a ship**.

– Show me **some wind**.

– I have **some wind**.

– Show me **more wind**.

– I have **more wind**.

– Ahhh! Ahhh!

听说活动

1. T: Guess what he will say?

T: Guess, what will happen next?

2. T: Let's listen to the whole passage and number the pictures.

(　　)

(　　)

(　　)

(　　)

3. Read out the story in roles.

4. T: Listen to the story and answer the following questions.
（可以用中文回答）

(1) Is Ma Liang a good boy?

(2) Why the old man gives the magic brush to Ma Liang?

(3) Why the bad man says: Ahhh!

(4) If you have a magic brush, what will you do?

(5) What do you learn from the story?

5. Act out the story.

课程设计者：珠海市香洲区第一小学 赵雨欣

《神笔马良》这篇小故事一年级的小朋友较为熟悉。它以连环画为基调，配上英文的听力文本，将故事与课本知识链接。故事情节编排合理有趣，能引发学生的阅读兴趣，给予其价值观的引导。

创编文本整合了适合学生学情的语言知识，在听说训练过程中，通过预测故事走向，以及创造信息差等活动使学生的语言学习能力和听说能力得到提高。

老师通过布置不同的任务提升学生的信息提取和整合能力。最后在让学生思考本文主旨的时候，鼓励学生积极思考，以取得良好的学习效果。

一年级主题 2　Body Organs

听力材料

The blind man: Ouch! What is it? Is it a wall?

Mr. Elephant: No, it's my **body**. I am Mr. Elephant.

The blind man: Hello. Mr. Elephant. Can I touch you?

Mr. Elephant: Sure, Let me show you my **face**! This is my **eye**. This is my **ear**. This is my **mouth**...

The blind man: Wow. It's so long. Is it a snake?

Mr. Elephant: No, it's my **nose**.

听说活动

1. Listen and choose.

(1) Who can you hear in the dialogue? (　　)

A. 

B. 

(2) The blind man "sees" __________. (　　)

A.

B.

(3) They are talking about_________. (　　)

A. school　　B. body organ　　C. fruit

2. Listen and circle .

Listen again and circle the part you hear.

3. Read and sing.

If you are happy and you know it, clap your hands.

If you are happy and you know it, touch your nose.

If you are happy and you know it, and you really want to show it.

If you are happy and you know it, touch your mouth.

If you are happy and you know it, ______________.

If you are happy and you know it,______________.

If you are happy and you know it, and you really want to show it.

If you are happy and you know it, ______________.

4. Let’s say.

Can you introduce yourself to your friends?

课程设计者：珠海市香洲区第一小学 周彤

听说活动 1：改编自成语故事“盲人摸象”。第一题将孩子们熟知的课本人物 Bill 与戴着眼镜的盲人做了鲜明的对比，为孩子们更好地理解下文做铺垫。第一、第二题让孩子们直面文本中的人物，更好地理解文本。第三题考察孩子的综合能力，提炼文本主要内容。

听说活动 2：通过让学生圈出所听到的内容，培养学生的综合能力，提高学生们的听力水平。

口语活动 3：通过简单的歌词改编，让学生轻松愉快地运用所学知识，提高学生的学习兴趣。

口语活动 4：结合文本，让孩子们灵活运用本单元的知识点。脸部的框架图让刚才输入的文本都能很好地得到输出，为孩子介绍脸部五官做了小提示。让孩子们意识到文本源于生活并且可以运用到生活中。有效地整合了本单元的知识点，提高了孩子们的听说能力和学习英语的兴趣。

一年级主题 3 Animals

听力材料

Lily: Mom, let's go to the zoo.

Mom: OK.

Lily: Wow! There are so many **animals**!

Lily: What's this?

Mom: Look at its tail. It's long. It's a **monkey**.

Lily: Ah! What's this? It's scary.

Mom: Look at its face. It's **a tiger**.

Mom: Look at that! It's flying.

Lily: It's **a bird**. I like birds!

What animals do you like?

听说活动

1. Listen and choose.

听力材料:

Lily: Wow! So many animals!

(1) Where are they? They are in the_____. (　　)

A. 

B. 

(2) What can you see in a zoo? I can see ____.(多选) (　　)

A. 　B. 　C. 　D. 　E. 

2. Listen and circle.

听力材料：

Lily: What's this?

Mom: Look at its tail. It's long.

(1) What's this? It's a (monkey / tiger).

听力材料：

Lily: Ah! What's this? It's scary!

(2) It's a big (tiger / cat).

听力材料：

Lily: Look at that! It's flying.

(3) It's a (cat / bird).

3. Listen and answer.

听力材料：

Lily: Mom, let's go to the zoo.

Mom: OK.

Lily: Wow! They are so many animals!

Lily: What's this?

Mom: Look at its tail. It's long. It's a monkey.

Lily: Ah! What's this? It's scary.

Mom: Look at its face. It's a tiger.

Mom: Look at that! It's flying.

Lily: It's a bird. I like birds!

(1) Lily likes____. (　　)

A. tigers　　B. birds

(2) They are talking about_____. (　　)

A. animals　B. colors　C. school

4. Speaking

What animals do you know? Can you introduce the animals?

课程设计者：珠海市香洲区南湾小学　欧小敏

语境化输入（Situated Input）对初学英语的孩子来说非常重要。将语言输入放到它合适的语境中去，使学生既能接触到要输入的语言，又能感受到这些材料出现的合适语境。

听说活动 1：通过孩子的对话，指明对话发生的地点是动物园。随后通过第二个问题让孩子思考在动物园能见到哪些动物，让孩子深入思考并不是所有动物都在动物园、分清家养动物与动物园动物的同时，激活孩子脑海中关于动物园的背景知识，让其从已有经验中提取相关信息，与将要学习的知识结合起来。

听说活动 2：主要是通过动物的一些特征，如尾巴很长、很吓人、会飞等关键特征，让孩子们凭借以往经验猜测动物。在这个过程中，孩子们的推理能力得到锻炼，思维品质得以提升。

听说活动 3：让孩子在听完完整对话后，归纳对话主题并留意细节信息。在这个过程中，孩子们的听力技巧、梳理和归纳能力都将得到训练。

口语活动 4：通过图片增强孩子们对动物图式的认知，之前的听力材料既提供了说的脚手架（图片和句型），降低了孩子们的认知难度，也为他们提供了发挥的空间，孩子们可根据自己的情况，进行口语表达，一句乃至一段话都可以。同时，孩子们的说也给聆听的孩子建立了说的模板，减缓了他们的认知焦虑。

一年级主题 4 Numbers

听力材料

I am Joy. I am **9** years old. I'm in Class **2**, Grade **3**. I like reading and writing. One day, two friends from the Big Tree School wrote me letters. It's a big surprise.

Part 1: Class begins.

Miss Wu: Boys and girls, please take out **a** pencil, **an** eraser and your English book.

Bill: Miss Wu, I am sorry. I can't find my schoolbag.

Lily: Bill. I have **5** pencils. Here is **a** pencil for you.

Bill: Thank you so much, Lily.

Andy: I have **4** erasers. I can give you one.

Bill: Thank you, Andy.

Miss Wu: I have **9** books on my desk. You can get one. You can call your mother after class, too.

Bill: Thank you, Miss Wu.

Part 2: After class.

Miss Wu: What's your mom's number?

Bill: My mom's number is **8–9–3–5–7–1–2**.

Miss Wu: **8–9–3–5–7–1–2**.

OK. I will call your mother after class.

Bill: Thank you very much.

听说活动

1. Listen to Part 1 and answer.

(1) Bill can't find his____. (　　)

A. 
B. 
C. 

(2) Miss Wu: Please take out________. (　　)

A. 
B. 
C. 

2. Listen and match.

Miss Wu　　Lily　　Andy

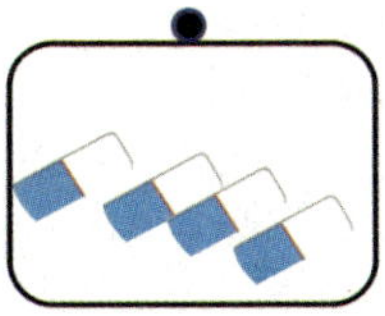

3. Listen to Part 2 and fill in the blanks.

Bill's mom's number is **8–__–3–5–__–1–2**.

4. Speaking: Make a phone book of the class.

Write down your number and share your number.

Try to write down your parents' or your friend's number.

Example:

Bill: Hello. My name is Bill. My number is 8–9–3–5–7–1–2.

课程设计者：珠海市香洲区南湾小学 欧小敏

本课听力材料的设计基于学生实际经验，从孩子找不到书包，到同学借给他文具和书本，让孩子抓住数字关键信息。在育人功能方面，听力文本的编写注重从日常生活入手，让孩子懂得同学之间应互相帮助，课前应准备好学习用品等。

说的活动从班级通讯录入手，让每个孩子都有机会去说自己（父母）的电话号码，孩子们也可以互相记录电话号码，锻炼孩子对数字的听辨能力。同时，在这个过程中，教师可教育孩子们谨记家长的联系电话，遇到紧急情况可以及时与家长取得联系。

一年级主题 5 Colors

听力材料

The Colorful Sky

Look at the sky! It has beautiful **colors**. In the morning, it's **yellow**! At noon, the sky is **blue** and **white**. But in the afternoon, the sky is **black**! It's going to rain. Let's go home! Now, look outside! A rainbow! It's **red**, **orange**, **yellow**, **green**, **blue**, and **purple**. I like the rainbow. I like the **colorful sky**!

听说活动

1. Listen and number.

(　　)　　(　　)　　(　　)　　(　　)

2. Listen and choose.

(1) What color is the sky in the morning? (　　)

A. black　　B. yellow　　C. blue

(2) What color is the sky at noon? (　　)

A. blue and white　B. red and white　C. blue and black

(3) It is raining, what color is the sky now? (　　)

A. yellow　　B. blue　　C. black

3.Listen and draw.

The sky is blue.

The tree is green.

The flower is red and yellow.

课程设计者：珠海市香洲区第五小学 朱翡霞

英语课程应成为学生发展技能、活跃思维等展现个性的过程。低年级学生的认知方式、语言习得、年龄等大体相同又存在个体差异，他们具有不同的学习需求和学习特点。在语言能力学段目标的习得和建构中，学生在听或看音视频材料时，能识别单词和日常熟悉事物，这也会为中高年级的习得与建构做铺垫。通过设计《五彩天空》这个听说课程，结合学生日常生活中看到的天空颜色和感受到的天空进行创编，颜色的视觉冲击和听说课程的集合，让学生一目了然，加深了他们对课程的理解。同时该文段与实际生活相结合，学生运用所学知识描述天空的颜色，不仅富有生活气息，还能引发他们强烈的学习兴趣。创编文本融合了科学知识，突出学科融合理念，注重语篇的学习，学生在进行“给短文排序、听问句选答语以及听描述画一画”等训练时，可以培养逻辑思维能力，将“听”和“思”结合起来。

听说活动 1：学生通过听完整的语篇，理解语篇的重要信息，能根据听到的词句识别图片，对图片进行排序。培养学生听力专注力的同时，激发学生的学习兴趣。

听说活动 2：学生通过活动 1 对语篇有了一定的理解，活动 2 是对本语篇理解的升华。学生通过阅读题目提取关键信息，可以培养观察与辨析的思维品质。

听说活动 3：学生经过了语篇的学习，进行迁移创新，通过听说活动创建属于自己的天空。

一年级主题 6 Fruits

听力材料

Delicious Fruit

I like **fruit**! I like eating **fruit**. **Apples** are red and sweet. They are yummy! **Bananas** are yellow and long. They are sweet. **Pears** are green and juicy. **Oranges** are orange. I put **apples**, **bananas**, **pears**, **oranges** and **watermelon** together. It's **fruit** salad! It's delicious!

听说活动

1. Listen and number.

______ → ______ → ______ →

______ → ______ → ______

(1)

(2)

(3)

(4)

(5)

2. Listen and choose.

(1) Apples are ____________. A. yellow　B. red

(2) Bananas are ___________. A. green　B. yellow

(3) Pears are _____________. A. orange　B. green

(4) Oranges are ___________. A. orange　B. red

3. Write and draw.

I like __________.

I like __________.

课程设计者：珠海市香洲区第五小学　朱翡霞

本课程设计秉持在体验中学习、在实践中运用、在迁移中创新的学习理念，倡导学生围绕真实情境和真实问题，激活已知，参与到指向主题意义探究的学习理解、应用实践和迁移创新等一系列相互关联、循环递进的语言学习和运用中。《美味的水果》这个故事是根据水果这一主题创编的，短文中的句子符合低年级学生的认知特点，简单易懂，朗朗上口。结合已知的颜色单词，运用所学知识描述水果的颜色同时也进行了相应的知识拓展内容。通过语篇排序，根据实际情况补充句子，培养学生的综合能力，提高学生的听力水平。同时促进学习能力的提升，有助于学生掌握科学的学习方法，养成良好的终身学习习惯。

听说活动 1：学生通过听完整的语篇，理解语篇的重要信息，在体验中学习，能根据听到的词句识别水果的图片，对图片进行排序。引导学生在学习理解中获取、梳理关键信息。

听说活动 2：引导学生在循环的语言学习和运用活动中，建立知识间的关联，培养学生良好的学习习惯和学习能力。

听说活动 3：学生经过了语篇的学习，进行迁移创新，根据主题设计自己喜欢的水果，然后进行交流，逐步形成语言意识，积累语言经验，进行有意义的沟通与交流。

一年级主题 7　Preposition of Place

听力材料

1. Mom: Look at this picture book. Where is Angel?

Lingling: She's **in** the schoolbag.

Lingling: Is the book **in** the schoolbag, too?

Mom: No, it's **on** the desk.

2. Lingling: What's this **in** the box, Mom?

Mom: It's a green pear. My good friend Yaoyao likes it.

Lingling: Look at the yellow banana, it's **on** the chair. Do you like it?

Mom: No, but Andy likes it very much. He wants to eat it.

3. Lingling: Look, the pencil case is **on** the desk.

Mom: Yes, but the red pencil is **in** the desk.

Lingling: Oh, I can see a lovely dog **under** the desk.

听说活动

1. Listen and choose.

听力材料

Mom: Look at this picture book. Where is Angel?

Lingling: She's in the schoolbag.

Lingling: Is the book in the schoolbag, too?

Mom: No, it's on the desk.

(1) Where is Angel?

A.  B.  C. 

(2) Where is the book?

A.  B.  C. 

听说活动

2. Listen and match.

听力材料

Lingling: What's this in the box, Mom?

Mom: It's a green pear. My good friend Yaoyao likes it.

Lingling: Look at the yellow banana, it's on the chair. Do you like it?

Mom: No, but Andy likes it very much. He wants to eat.

(1) 

(2) 

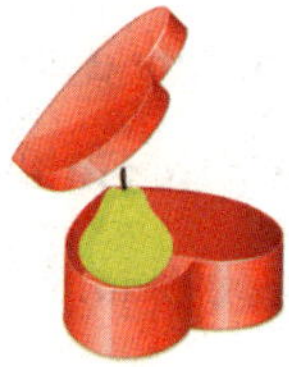

听说活动

3.Listen and match.

听力材料

Lingling: Look, the pencil case is on the desk.

Mom: Yes, but the red pencil is in the desk.

Lingling: Oh, I can see a lovely dog under the desk.

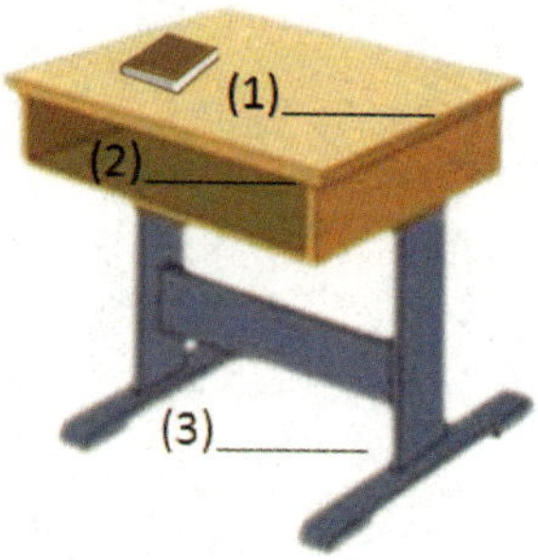

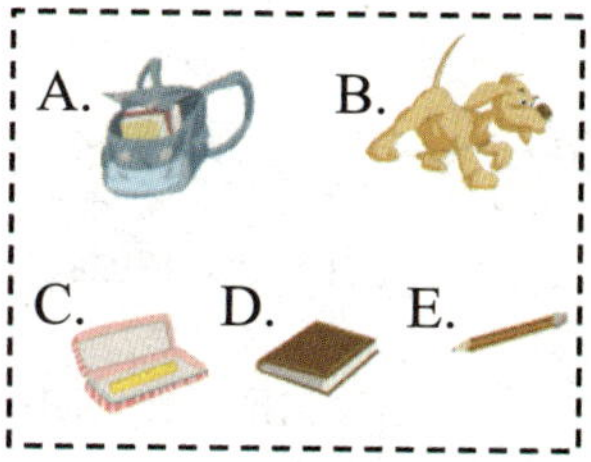

听说活动

4. Listen and write.

听力材料

Mom: Look at this picture book. Where is Angel?

Lingling: She's **in** the schoolbag.

Lingling: Is the book **in** the schoolbag, too?

Mom: No, it's **on** the desk.

Lingling: What's this **in** the box, Mom?

Mom: It's a green pear. My good friend Yaoyao likes it.

Lingling: Look at the yellow banana, it's **on** the chair. Do you like it?

Mom: No, but Andy likes it very much. He wants to eat.

Lingling: Look, the pencil case is **on** the desk.

Mom: Yes, but the red pencil is **in** the desk.

Lingling: Oh, I can see a lovely dog **under** the desk.

(1) Lingling is talking with______(Mom Dad).

(2) Angel is______(on in) the schoolbag and the book is on the______ (chair desk).

(3) Yaoyao likes the______(green yellow) pear.

(4) The dog is______(in on under) the desk.

课程设计者：珠海市香洲区广昌小学 姚丽芬

听说活动 1：此活动以图片的形式呈现本课容易混淆的方位词，加强表达位置的功能句在恰当的情境中运用。通过引导学生先看图片，再根据图片预测听力内容来降低难度，培养学生的观察和空间想象能力。对话和图片的设计比较直观和有趣，学生做起来比较容易，有利于建立学习英语的自信心，提升学习英语的兴趣。

听说活动 2：学生通过听对话，找出 Yaoyao 和 Andy 喜欢的水果，并连线。通过这项活动，学生在情境中感知、理解、运用语言知识，培养获取信息的能力和运用语言的能力。同时复习之前学过的水果等词，并进一步熟悉教材的主要人物，为后面主题的学习打下坚实的基础。

听说活动 3：通过前面的活动，学生对方位词已有了一定的了解，同时对物品位置的英语表达也比较熟练。此活动通过倾听并感知情景，让学生选出具体位置的物品，培养学生的专注力，以及在真实情境中理解、思考、推理、运用语言的能力，从而培养学生综合运用语言的能力。

听说活动 4：前面三个活动的练习是基于图片来设计的，此活动设计难度加大，让学生通过听对话选词，帮助学生充分理解单词的意义。同时，学生已经熟知如何询问和描述物品的位置，让他们再次听完整对话，然后归纳谈话主题并筛选出关键信息，可以有效训练他们的听力技巧和归纳能力。

一年级主题 8 Garfield House

听力材料

1. Garfield moved to a new house. What's in the house? Listen and tick.

This is the light **near** the bed. This is the bed **near** the door.

This is the door **near** the box. What's **behind** the box?

2. What's in Garfield's new house? Listen and number the pictures.

This is the light **near** the bed. This is the bed **near** the door.

This is the door **near** the box. What's **behind** the box?

3. What's in Garfield's new house? Listen and choose.

(1) What's **behind** the door? A chair.

(2) What's **near** the light? A cat.

4. Garfield likes to play hide-and-seek in the house. Where is Garfield? Listen and number the pictures.

Garfield is under the table. Garfield is under the bed.

Garfield is behind the chair. Garfield is near the light.

Garfield is in the cupboard. Garfield is on the light.

Oh! Garfield! You naughty cat!

听说活动

1. Listen and tick.

听力材料

Garfield moved to a new house. What's in the house? Listen and tick.

This is the light near the bed. This is the bed near the door.

This is the door near the box. What's behind the box?

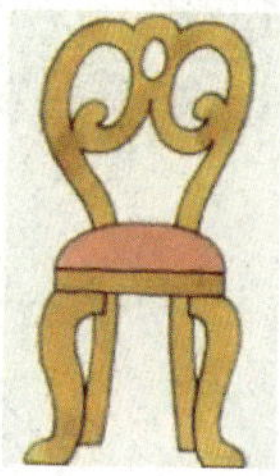
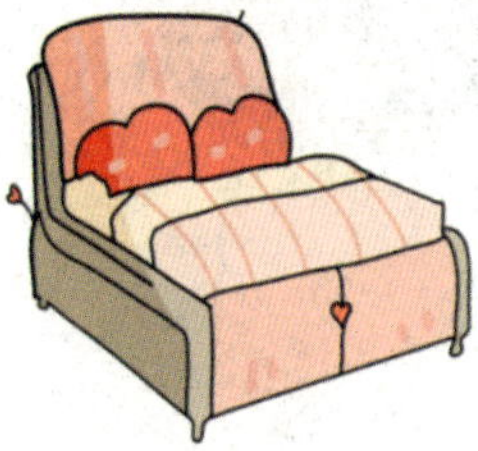
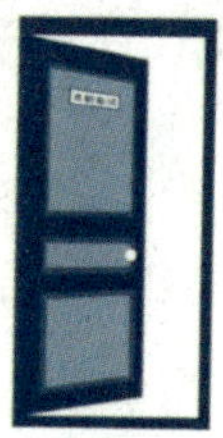

(√)　　( )　　( )　　( )　　( )

2. Listen and number.

听力材料

What's in Garfield's new house? Listen and number the pictures.

This is the light near the bed. This is the bed near the door.

This is the door near the box. What's behind the box?

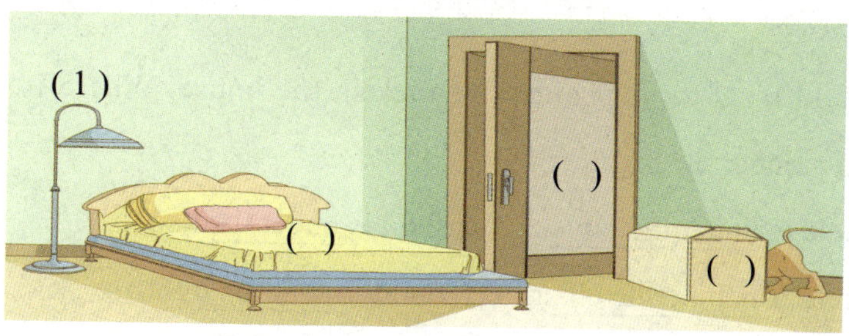

3. Look and say. “This is the ... near the ...”

4. Listen and choose.

听力材料

What’s in Garfield’s new house? Listen and choose.

(1) What’s behind the door? A chair.

(2) What’s near the light? A cat.

(1) What’s behind the door? (   )

A.  B.  C. 

(2) What’s near the light? (   )

A.  B.  C. 

5. Listen and number.

听力材料

Garfield likes to play hide-and-seek in the house. Where is Garfield? Listen and number the pictures.

Garfield is under the table.   Garfield is under the bed.

Garfield is behind the chair.   Garfield is near the light.

Garfield is in the cupboard. Garfield is on the light.

Oh! Garfield! You naughty cat!

(1)

( )

( )

(1)

( )

( )

6. Look and say.

“ Where is Garfield? Garfield is ...”

课程设计者：珠海市香洲区拱北小学 李世勤

听说素材通过谈论 Garfield 的新房子，以及四个听说活动和两个看图说话活动展开。

听说活动 1：以图片的形式呈现房间内物品及方位词，引导学生先看图片，再根据听力内容勾选出听到的内容，培养学生的观察能力和逻辑思维能力。

听力活动 2：以综合图的形式呈现房间物品和方位关系，通过听录音给图片具体位置的物品排序，培养学生的理解、思考和推理能力。

听说活动 3：让学生根据图片方位，进行口语交际，培养他们运用语言的能力。

听说活动 4：以图片的形式呈现容易混淆的方位词，通过引导学生先看图片，再根据图片预测听力内容，来降低听力难度，培养学生的观察能力、空间想象能力和逻辑思维能力。这部分对话和图片设计也比较直观和有趣，学生做起来比较容易。

听说活动 5 和 6：通过前四个活动的练习，学生更加熟悉询问和描述物品的位置，让孩子再次听完整对话，然后归纳谈话主题并筛选出关键信息。在这个过程中，学生的听力技巧和归纳能力得到有效训练。故事的情节编排合理有趣，在激发学生兴趣的同时，给予其价值观的引导。

一年级主题 9　Toys

听力材料

Hello. I am Binbin. I'm a boy. I am from China. I collect the glass balls. What color are the balls? Some are yellow. Some are blue. Some are green. Oh! Where is my green ball? It's in the desk. Do you like my toys? Let's play together.

听说活动

1. T: Listen to the passage and choose the right topic. (　　)

A. Room

B. Toys

C. Fruit

2. T: What toys does Binbin have? (　　)

A. glass balls

B. doll

C. toy car

3.T: What color are the balls? Please circle the right colors.

4. T: Is Binbin a boy? Please choose the right answer. (　　)

A. Yes, he is.　　　　　B. No, he isn't.

5. T: Where is Binbin's green ball? (　　)

A.　　　　　B.　　　　　C.

6. T: Do you want to play with Binbin together? (　　)

A. Yes, I do.　　　　　B. No, I don't.

课程设计者：珠海市香洲区第一小学　李玉莲

讨论玩具是小学生非常喜欢的话题。听力文本讲述 Binbin 喜欢的一种玩具——玻璃珠，并通过介绍玻璃珠的颜色等表达对玩具的热爱。文本的编写符合一年级下册学生的认知规律，介绍的是 20 世纪 80 年代儿童的玩具，简单有趣，富有时代感。

创编的文本结合一年级多个主题的知识点，包括 I have⋯, colors, Where is ⋯，培养学生英语知识的综合运用能力。听说是英语学习的重要方法，建议在使用文本时，教师适当介绍玩具的背景，并出示图片，结合语言材料进行提问等，达到激发学生学习兴趣和动机的教学目的。教师通过语境教学，采用听说演思等方式，引导学生积极参与，大胆表达，听别人喜欢的，说自己热爱的，从而提高小学生初步运用英语的能力，真正做到把所学知识活用到生活当中。

一年级主题 10 Food

听力材料

Binbin: Mom, I'm hungry.

Mom: It's time for dinner!

Binbin: Oh, **fish**! I like it!

Mom: This is for you, Binbin.

Binbin: I love you, mom.

Mom: Do you want **vegetables**?

Binbin: Yes, I do. It's yummy!

Mom: Do you want **chicken**?

Binbin: Yes, of course.

Mom: Do you want **eggs**?

Binbin: No, I don't. Can I have **rice**?

Mom: Sure.

Binbin: Yeah!

Mom: I'm hungry, too. I want **vegetables**.

Binbin: Let's share!

听说活动

1. Listen and tick.

(1) Binbin is _______.

(2) Binbin likes _______.

(3) Binbin doesn't (不) like _______.

(4) Mom wants _______.

2. Listen and choose.

A

B

C

D

E

F

G

H

(　)(　)(　)(　)(　)

3. Draw a menu.

I want ...

课程设计者：珠海市香洲区广昌小学 杨春薇

听力材料中的场景是日常生活中经常出现的小朋友与家人共进晚餐，Binbin和妈妈在饭桌上以“你喜欢吃什么”和“你是否想吃什么”为话题展开对话，属于人与社会的范畴。Binbin是课本上的人物，也是一年级学生相当熟悉的小伙伴了，听他和妈妈的对话就像是在听朋友和他的妈妈对话，能给学生更好的代入感，同时也能减轻对说话者的陌生感，使其快速联系到自己的日常生活，帮助其理解听力内容。

编造的对话涉及一年级上册和下册部分的内容，能够唤起学生对已学知识的记忆，同时联系本单元的内容，为他们在日常生活中运用语言增添词汇量，给语言者搭建起一个框架，使他们能做到“有话可说”。

设计的听说活动主要以辨别图片信息为主，有利于学生更好地联系具体的图片去认知单词，也减轻了他们的记忆负担。记忆单词一直是英语学习的一个难点，即学生无法建立语言文字和实物间的联系。学生通过分辨不同的图片，可以增强对文字的理解，加深印象。

在完成听说活动后，学生需要做一个输出的活动，即根据自身的喜好设计一份菜单。菜单以绘画的方式为主，降低了难度，也能较好地吸引学生的兴趣、激发他们的创作热情。

一年级主题 11　Drink

听力材料

Joy: Mike, happy birthday!

Mike: Thank you!

Joy: Let's have a party!

Everyone: Hooray!

Mike: Look! What's on the desk?

Joy: Juice, **milk** and **cola**.

Mike: Yes. Do you want some **juice**?

Joy: Yes, please.

Mike: Andy, do you want some juice?

Andy: No, thanks. I want some **milk**.

Mike: Here you are. Lily, do you want **juice**?

Lily: No, thanks. I want some **cola**.

Mike: Here you are.

Lily: Thank you.

Joy: It's song time. Let's sing together!

配上《两只老虎》的伴奏。

Happy birthday, happy birthday.

Juice for you, **juice** for you.

I like **juice**, I like **juice**, thank you, thank you.

Happy birthday, happy birthday.

Milk for you, **milk** for you.

I like **milk**, I like **milk**, thank you, thank you.

听说活动

1. Look, guess and circle.

A. Thank you.

B. Hello!

A. Let’s run.

B. Let’s have a party.

A. Juice.

B. Apple.

2. Look and match.

juice　　milk　　tea　　water

3. Let's sing.

Model:

Happy birthday, happy birthday.

Juice  for you, juice  for you.

I like juice , I like juice , thank you, thank you.

Happy birthday, happy birthday.

Milk  for you, milk  for you.

I like milk , I like milk , thank you, thank you.

Happy birthday, happy birthday.

___ for you, ___ for you.

I like ___, I like ___, thank you, thank you.

Happy birthday, happy birthday.

___ for you, ___ for you.

I like ______, I like ______, thank you, thank you.

课程设计者：珠海市香洲区广昌小学　杨春薇

通过庆祝 Mike 的生日引出孩子们一起举办生日派对的场景，属于人与社会的范畴。这样的生活场景能够较好地激发学生的兴趣、提高他们的参与热情，同时引导学生联想派对上可能会出现的事物，比如食物和饮料等。接着联系前面单元学习到的方位词，询问桌子上有什么饮料，既复习了所学的词汇，又进一步明确了听力材料的主题。通过 Mike 和不同的朋友的问答活动来操练重点句型，能有效帮助学生把听力内容的理解单位从单词变成句子，也能帮助他们理解这些话语在日常生活中的使用范围。

第一个听说活动是通过观察图片和场景，猜测里面可能出现的对话内容和相关信息。接着通过听录音辅助理解，进而把句子圈出来，既考验了学生的观察和预测能力，也锻炼了他们听取相关信息的能力；第二个活动是根据所学知识把饮料的单词和图片匹配并连线，目的是激发学生已有的知识储备，与此同时把文本信息和听力材料对应起来；最后学生需要根据例子自己加以创造，输出一首 *chant*，检验学习成果，并加深对句型的印象。

一年级主题 12 Clothes

听力材料

Joy: Can I have new **clothes**?

Mom: Sure. Let's go to the shop.

Joy: Wow! There are so many beautiful **clothes**.

Mom: Look at the yellow **T-shirt**.

Joy: I like the yellow **T-shirt**.

Mom: Look at the **skirt.** It's blue.

Joy: I like the blue **skirt**, too.

Joy: What's near the blue **skirt**?

Mom: It's a red **dress**.

Joy: I like the **dress** best!

Mom: Try on the **dress**, it looks nile on you.

Joy: Wow, I'm beautiful now!

听力活动

1. Listen and choose.

(1) Where are Joy and Mom ? They are in a _____. (   )

A. 

B. 

听力材料：

Joy: Can I have new clothes?

Mom: Sure. Let's go to the shop.

Joy: Wow! There are so many beautiful clothes.

(2) What do they see in the shop? Please circle the right pictures. (多选题)

A. 

B. 

C. 

D. 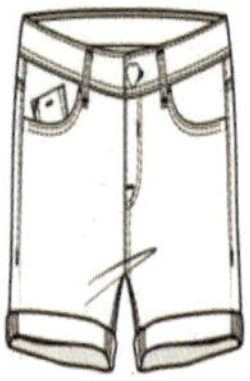

E. 

F. 

听力材料：

Mom: Look at the yellow <u>**T-shirt**</u>.

Joy: I like the yellow T-shirt.

Mom: Look at the <u>**skirt**</u>. It's blue.

Joy: I like the blue skirt, too.

Joy: What's near the blue skirt?

Mom: It’s a red dress.

Joy: I like the dress best!

Mom: Try on the **dress**, it looks nile on you.

Joy: Wow, I’m beautiful now!

2. Listen to the dialogue again.

(1) Match and color.

(2) Choose the right picture.

What’s near the skirt? It’s a red __________. (T–shirt / dress)

听力材料

Mom: Look at the **yellow** T–shirt.

Joy: I like the **yellow** T–shirt.

Mom: Look at the skirt. It's **blue**.

Joy: I like the **blue** skirt, too.

Joy: What's near the blue skirt?

Mom: It's a **red dress**.

Joy: I like the dress best!

3. Listen and choose.

(1) Joy likes________ best. (　　)

A. T-shirt　　　　B. skirt　　　　C. dress

(2) They are talking about________ . (　　)

A. toys　　　　B. clothes　　　　C. food

4. Let's say.

Design your clothes shop and introduce your clothes to us!

课程设计者：珠海市杨匏安纪念学校　苏明慧

针对低年级学生的学习及认知特点，英语课堂需要大量的语言输入，才能促进语言的输出。另外，美国语言学家 Krashen 提出的可理解输入假设理论（Comprehensible Input Hypothesis）认为，人们习得语言的必要条件和关键是接收“可理解的输入”。因此，英语教师要在可理解性的输入上下功夫，创造更优质的输入，并围绕语境进行多样化的教学活动，让学生利用语境和原有的知识储备理解输入。

本节听说课创编的文本以本单元重点单词和句型为基础，结合主题 8 和主题 9，以及一年级上学期的知识，让学生借助已学知识来理解听力文本。在听说融合的教学活动中，学生能掌握理解文本、获取细节信息的能力，听后的问题促进学生知识的深度加工，以便在输出环节学生能利用听力文本中的句型进行口语表达，对知识进行迁移内化。

听说活动 1：指明了对话发生的地点，让学生明白对话是在何种语境下产生，激活学生原有知识，推进接下来的听力文本理解。随后学生需要提取对话中出现的关键词，圈出服装店中她们谈论的衣服，该活动能让学生快速捕捉与语境相关的词汇，加深对语境的理解。

听说活动 2：在原有文本基础上，让学生获取更多细节，例如颜色和物体的位置。在此过程中，任务环环相扣，新旧知识融合，学生的概括总结能力也得到提升。

听说活动 3：学生在听完整段对话后，把已发现的细节信息与听力文本主题结合起来。在这个过程中，深化了学生对主题的理解，丰富了他们的知识结构。

听说活动 4：进行听力的输入后，学生要利用听力文本的相关句型，去设计和谈论他们心目中的服装店，有效进行了知识的迁移应用。学生的发散性思维及创造性思维得以发展，语言综合运用能力得到训练。

二年级主题 1 My Family

听力材料

1. Girl: Hi!

Boy: Hello! Welcome!

Girl: Thank you.

Girl: What's this?

Boy: It's a photo of my **family**. There are seven people in my **family**.

Girl: Wow! What a big **family**!

2. Girl: Ah! I can see you. I like your yellow T-shirt.

Boy: Thank you.

3. Girl: Who is she?

Boy: She is my **sister**.

Girl: I like her red dress.

4. Girl: Who is he? The man with brown hair?

Boy: He is my **father**.

5. Boy: Look! This is my **mother**.

Girl: Ah! She is wearing a green shirt!

Boy: And the little boy is my **brother**.

Girl: So cute!

6. Boy : Who is she? She is wearing a pink shirt.

Girl : She is my **grandmother**.

7. Boy : Look at the man! He has a big nose.

Girl : Oh, this is my **grandfather**.

听说活动

1. Listen and choose.

听力材料

Boy: It's a photo of my **family**.

(1) What are they talking about? They are talking about_____. (　　)

A.

B.

听力材料

Boy: There are seven people in my family.

(2) How many people are there in the boy's family? (　　)

A. five　　B. six　　C. seven

2. Listen, guess and circle, guess and circle.

听力材料

Girl: Ah! I can see you. I like your yellow T–shirt.

Boy: Thank you.

(1) Which one is the boy?

听力材料

Girl: Who is she?

Boy: She is my **sister**.

Girl: I like her red dress.

(2) Which one is the boy's sister?

听力材料

Girl: Who is he? The man with brown hair?

Boy: He is my **father**.

(3) Which one is the boy's father?

听力材料

Boy: Look! This is my **mother**.

Girl: Ah! She is wearing a green shirt!

Boy: And the little boy is my **brother**.

Girl: So cute!

(4) Which one is the boy’s mother? And little brother?

听力材料

Boy : Who is she? She is wearing a pink shirt.

Girl : She is my **grandmother**.

(5) Which one is the boy’s grandmother?

听力材料

Boy : Look at the man! He has a big nose.

Girl : Oh, this is my **grandfather**.

(6) Which one is the boy's grandfather?

3. Listen and number.

4. Let's say.

How many people are there in your family? Who are they?

For example:

课程设计者：珠海市斗门区齐正小学 谢音

初学英语的孩子需要用熟悉的事物来接受新知，正所谓以旧带新，这样才有可能激活他们脑海中储存的图式，从而掌握新知，并实现输出的目标。二年级主题 1 是家庭成员，是孩子们比较熟悉的话题。对话围绕介绍家庭成员照片展开，融合了五官、数字、颜色、服饰的英文表达，以旧带新，激活孩子们关于家庭成员的图式。

听说活动 1：通过男孩的话，指明对话主要内容是介绍家人。随后通过第二个问题让孩子思考对话中的男孩有几个家庭成员，让孩子回顾数字对应的英文表达；同时激活孩子脑海中关于家庭成员的背景知识，从已有经验中提取相关信息，与即将学习的知识产生联结。

听说活动 2：主要是通过男孩与女孩的对话，以一年级学过的 face 和 colors 和 clothes 为线索找出男孩的家人。在这个过程中，孩子们的推理能力得到锻炼，训练了孩子们的思维品质。

听说活动 3：让孩子在听完完整对话后，为对话中先后提到的家庭成员排序。在这个过程中，孩子们的梳理归纳能力得到有效训练。

口语活动 4：通过画画这一活动激发孩子们的表达兴趣，而之前的听力材料为孩子们的口头表达搭好了脚手架，降低了孩子们的认知难度。同时，孩子们的口头表达也给聆听的孩子提供了参考，让他们有所准备。

二年级主题 2 Boys and Girls

听力材料

1. Mom: Thank you for taking me to your school canteen, Bob.

Bob: You are welcome, mom. It's 12 O'clock. What do you want to eat?

Mom: I want some noodles and vegetables. How about you?

Bob: I want some rice and chicken.

2. Mom: Oh, look at the boys and girls over there, are they your classmates?

Bob: Yes, we are all in class 3.

Mom: Well, look at that boy. He is wearing a green T-shirt. What's his name?

Bob: His name is George. He is my good friend.

3. Mom: How about the girl near George? What's her name? She is drinking milk.

Bob: Her name is Lily. She has long black hair and two big eyes. She's my friend, too.

4. Mom: And who is that man? He is wearing a black shirt.

Bob: He's our English teacher, Mr. Green. We all like him.

5. Mom: Is that woman your teacher, too? She is wearing a blue dress.

Bob: Yes. She is Miss White. She's our Chinese teacher.

听说活动

1. T: Listen and choose. (part1)

听力材料

Mom: Thank you for taking me to your school canteen, Bob.

Bob: You are welcome, mom. It's 12 O'clock. What do you want to eat?

Mom: I want some noodles and vegetables. How about you?

Bob: I want some rice and chicken.

(1) Where are Bob and his mother? They're in a_________. (　　)

A. 

B. 

(2) What do you want for lunch? I want __________ for lunch. (　　)

A. 

B. 

C 

D. 

E. 

F. 

G. 

H. 

2.T: Listen and choose.(part2)

听力材料

Mom: Oh, look at the boys and girls over there, are they your classmates?

Bob: Yes, we are all in class 3.

Mom: Oh, look at that boy. He is wearing a green T-shirt. What's his name?

Bob: His name is George. He likes chicken and juice. He is my good friend.

(1) Who's George? (　　)

A. 

B. 

听力材料

Mom: How about the girl near George? What's her name? She is drinking milk.

Bob: Her name is Lily. She has long black hair and two big eyes. She's my friend, too.

(2) Who's Lily? (　　)

A. 

B. 

3. T: Listen and choose. (part3)

听力材料

Mom: Thank you for taking me to your school canteen, Bob.

Bob: You are welcome, mom. It’s 12 O’clock. What do you want to eat?

Mom: I want some noodles and vegetables. How about you?

Bob: I want some rice and chicken.

Mom: Oh, look at the boys and girls over there, are they your friends?

Bob: Yes, we are all in class 3.

Mom: Well, look at that boy. He is wearing a green T-shirt. What’s his name?

Bob: His name is George. He is my best friend.

Mom: How about the girl near George? What’s her name? She is drinking milk.

Bob: Her name is Lily. She has a long black hair and two big eyes. She’ s my friend, too.

Mom: And who is that man? He is wearing a black shirt.

Bob: He’s our English teacher, Mr. Green. We all like him.

Mom: Is that woman your teacher, too? She is wearing a blue dress.

Bob: Yes. She is Miss White. She’s our Chinese teacher.

(1) Mr. Green is wearing a ______. (   )

A.

B.

(2) They are talking about ______. (　　)

A.

B.

4. Let's say.

Do you have a good friend? Please draw a picture of your friend and introduce him/her .

My good friend

课程设计者：珠海市斗门区齐正小学　杨傲

本课聚焦学生身边的人物介绍，听力内容围绕妈妈和Bob一起走进学校食堂用餐，听Bob介绍自己的朋友展开。对话融合了食物、饮料、服装等在一年级学过的旧知。这种真实的语言情境对于刚学习英语一年的学生来说非常重要，它能调动学生已有的生活经验，激发学生的学习兴趣，降低学生的听说难度。

听说活动1：通过妈妈和Bob的对话，指明对话发生的地点是学校的食堂。Canteen这个词虽然孩子们没有学过，可是可以根据信息12 O'clock， noodles and vegetables，rice and chicken 推断出来地点是学校食堂。

随后通过第二个问题让孩子思考午餐自己想吃什么，联系学生的实际，调动孩子一年级时学过食物和饮料主题的知识，和即将学习的知识产生联系。

听说活动 2：通过人物的特点，比如身着绿色 T 恤、有着黑色长发和大眼睛等，根据图片来判断人物特性，引导学生有意识地去关注不同人物的区别，训练学生听取关键信息的能力，提升听力的技巧。

听说活动 3：让孩子重听完整对话后，学会捕捉文章的细节信息，归纳出对话人物讨论的主题。学生捕捉关键词、梳理和归纳信息的能力得到了训练。

口语活动 4：通过绘画好朋友的照片激活孩子们关于朋友的图式，让学生能联系生活实际，结合在听力对话中听到的单词和句型，对自己的好朋友进行姓名、服装、想吃的食物等方面的描述。

二年级主题 3 My Friends

听力材料

Bill: Mom, I'm drawing a picture.

Mom: Wow! There are so many boys and girls. Who are they?

Bill: They are my friends.

Mom: Who is she?

Bill: She is Cindy. **She is short**.

Mom: Who is he? **He is tall**.

Bill: He is Tom. **He is big**, too.

Mom: Who is she?

Bill: She is Joy. **She is thin**.

Mom: You have so many friends!

Bill: Yes. And I love them all.

What about your friends? Can you introduce them?

听说活动

1. Listen and choose.

听力材料

Bill: Mom, I'm drawing a picture.

Mom: Wow! There are so many boys and girls. Who are they?

Bill: They are my friends.

(1) What can you see in Bill's picture? I can see____________. (　　)

A. 

B. 

2. Listen and circle.

听力材料

Mom: Who is she?

Bill: She is Cindy. She is short.

(1) Who is Cindy? (　　)

A. 

B. 

听力材料

Mom: Who is he? He is tall.

Bill: He is Tom. He is big, too.

(2) Who is Tom? (　　)

A. 

B. 

听力材料

Mom: Who is she?

Bill: She is Joy. She is thin.

(3) Who is Joy? (　　)

A.

B.

3. Listen and answer.

听力材料

Bill: Mom, I'm drawing a picture.

Mom: Wow! There are so many boys and girls. Who are they?

Bill: They are my friends.

Mom: Who is she?

Bill: She is Cindy. She is short.

Mom: Who is he? He is tall.

Bill: He is Tom. He is big, too.

Mom: Who is she?

Bill: She is Joy. She is thin.

Mom: You have so many friends!

Bill: Yes. And I love them all.

(1) Tom is ______. (　　)

A. short and thin B. tall and big

(2) They are talking about_____. ( )

A. friends B. animals C. school

4. Let's say.

Do you love your friends? Can you introduce your friends?

课程设计者：珠海市斗门区齐正小学 蔡少娥

听是学生获得信息和语言输入的主要途径，是理解性技能。对于初学英语的学生来说，在主题语境中，感知、体验、积累和运用主题语言，在解读听力语篇中训练听说策略，能促进语言知识和听说技能的协同发展。有效的听说活动能将听和说相融合，让学生在语言输入的基础上进行内化，并在具体的语境中进行表达。

本课的主题是“我的朋友”，属于新课标中“人与社会”的范畴。本段听力材料创设了 Tom 与妈妈的对话，在对话中融入本单元重点的句型和词汇，帮助学生感知和体验语言。

听说活动 1：通过孩子和妈妈的对话表明对话内容有关朋友。通过第一个问题让学生思考 Bill 的画里会有什么，训练孩子们边听边猜测语篇主题的技能。图片可以帮助孩子们理解 friends 的含义，也让他们巩固了 friends 一词的发音与意义的联系。

听说活动 2：主要是通过人物的一些特征，如矮的、高的、瘦的，让孩子们将听到的重点词汇的发音与意义联系起来，同时根据图片做出转化与判断。这一听说活动训练了学生获取信息和理解信息的能力。

听说活动 3：让孩子在听完完整对话后，归纳谈话主题并留意细节信息。在这个过程中，孩子们的听力技巧、梳理和归纳能力得到有效训练。同时对孩子情感意识进行渗透——要爱自己的朋友。

口语活动 4：通过图片激活孩子们关于朋友的图式，之前的听力材料既提供了说的脚手架（图片和句型），降低了孩子们的认知难度，也提供了发挥的空间，孩子们可以根据自己的情况，进行口语表达说一句乃至一段话都可以。同时，之前的听说活动也给聆听的孩提供了说的模板，减轻了他们的认知焦虑。

二年级主题 4　In the Community

听力材料

Bill: Mom, today is Saturday. It's sunny. Where are we going?

Mom: We are going to the **park**.

Bill: Wow, what a beautiful **park**!

Mom: There are some trees and flowers in the park.

Bill: Mum, look! The trees over there are pretty tall.

Mom: Oh I see. What color are they?

Bill: They're green.

Bill: There are some beautiful flowers. Can I pick them?

Mom: No, we shouldn't pick the flowers in the park.

They are going to the **supermarket** after that. In the **supermarket**...

Bill: Mom, can I buy some cakes? They look delicious!

Mom: Sure. How many cakes would you like?

Bill: Thank you. I want to buy five cakes and share with my good friend Andy. He likes cakes!

听说活动

1. Listen and choose.

Bill: Mom, today is Saturday. It's sunny. Where are we going?

Mom: We are going to the park.

(1) Where are they going? They are going to the______________. (　　)

A. 

B. 

(2) What can Bill see in the park? He can see_________.(多选题)(　　)

A.  B.  C.  D.  E. 

2. Listen, guess and circle.

Bill: Mum, look! The trees over there are pretty tall.

(1) Are the trees tall?

(Yes / No).

Bill: There are some beautiful flowers. Can I pick them?

Mom: No, we shouldn't pick the flowers in the park.

(2) Can we pick some flowers in the park?

(Yes/No).

Bill: Mum, look! The trees over there are pretty tall.

Mom: Oh I see. What color are they?

Bill: They're green.

(3) What color are the trees?

They're (green/ blue).

3. Listen and answer.

Bill: Mom, today is Saturday. It's sunny. Where are we going?

Mom: We are going to the park.

Bill: Wow, what a beautiful park!

Mom: There are some trees and flowers in the park.

Bill: Mum, look! The trees over there are pretty tall.

Mom: Oh I see. What color are they?

Bill: They're green.

Bill: There are some beautiful flowers. Can I pick them?

Mom: No, we shouldn't pick the flowers in the park.

They are going to the supermarket after that. In the supermarket...

Bill: Mom, Can I buy some cakes? They look delicious!

Mom: Sure. How many cakes would you like?

Bill: Thank you. I want to buy five cakes and share with my good friend Andy. He likes cakes!

(1) Bill wants to buy ____cakes. (　　)

A. six　　　B. five.

(2) Is Andy in the park? _____. (　　)

A. Yes, he is.　　　B. No, he isn't.　　　C. We don't know.

4. Let's say.

Where are you going on Saturdays? Can you introduce some other places?

课程设计理念：珠海市斗门区齐正小学 梁景珊

本课的内容选取了贴近日常生活的一些地点，学生对本单元的核心词汇都非常熟悉。听力文本根据本单元的核心词汇和句型创造语境，并结合一二年级学过的大量词汇，学生在听时能快速捕捉主题内容，从而选出正确答案。

文本创设了多个Bill和母亲的对话，以“今天是星期六，我们要去哪里玩”为切入点，展开了后面的对话。五段对话中不但融入了本单元的核心词汇和句型，而且加入了一、二年级学过的词汇和句型。在听说训练中，听取重要信息，有利于锻炼学生的逻辑思维能力，提高他们的语言学习能力和听说能力。

听说活动设置了干扰选项，都是以前学过的知识。学生在做题过程中不仅复习了旧知识点，又巩固了新知识，并进行深刻的思考、总结和表达。听说活动，提高了学生的思维和概括能力。

二年级主题 5 In the Park

听力材料

1.

Bill: Good morning, Andy.

Andy: Good morning, Bill.

Bill: Where are you going?

Andy: I am going to the park.

Bill: Where is the park?

Andy: It's near our school. It's a new park.

Bill: Wow! Let's go together, shall we?

Andy: OK.

2.

Bill: Wow! What a big park!

Andy: Look. Some boats are on the lake.

Bill: One, two, three…There are seven boats.

3.

Andy: There are many flowers on the grass.

Bill: Let's pick some flowers. My mother likes flowers.

Andy: No, you can't do that.

Bill: I am so sorry. I should buy flowers in the shop.

听说活动

1. Listen and choose.

听力材料

Bill: Good morning, Andy.

Andy: Good morning, Bill.

Bill: Where are you going?

Andy: I am going to the park.

Bill: Where is the park?

Andy: It's near our school. It's a new park.

Bill: Wow! Let's go together, shall we?

Andy: OK.

(1) Where is Andy going? He is going to the ________. ( )

A. 

B. 

(2) Where is the park? The park is near the ________. ( )

A. 

B. 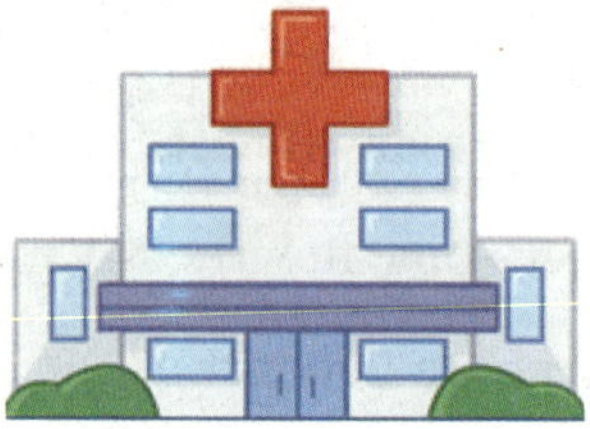

2. Listen and judge.

听力材料

Bill: Wow! What a big park!

Andy: It's so beautiful. Some boats are on the lake.

Bill: One, two, three…There are seven boats.

(1) The park is big and beautiful. (　　)

(2) There are three boats on the lake. (　　)

听力材料

Andy: There are many flowers on the grass.

Bill: Let's pick some flowers. My mother likes flowers.

Andy: No, you can't do that.

Bill: I am so sorry. I should buy flowers in the shop.

(3) Andy sees some trees on the grass. (　　)

(4) Andy and Bill can pick some flowers in the park. (　　)

3. Let's say.

Do you like to go to the park?

What can you see in the park?

课程设计者：珠海市斗门区齐正小学 黄洁萍

In the Park 主要聚焦公园这个话题，学习公园里有哪些常见的事物，学会用 There be 句型（表示某地有某物）。听力材料围绕 Bill 和 Andy 一起去新公园游玩展开，不仅涉及新词汇和句型，还复现了和方位词、数词等相关内容，既能巩固旧知识，又能训练新知识。在对话的最后，Bill 提议摘一束鲜花送给妈妈，Andy 制止了他这种不爱护环境的行为，起到教育学生环境保护的作用。

听说活动 1：通过 Bill 和 Andy 的对话，指明人物即将前往的地点是公园和公园的位置，引导学生复习巩固和社区活动场所有关的英文表达，以及建筑物位置的表达方式。激活学生脑海中关于公园的背景知识，让他们从已有经验中提取相关信息，为接下来的学习活动做准备。

听说活动 2：通过听 Bill 和 Andy 的两段对话，让学生判断句子的正误。考查的是学生提取信息和留意细节信息的能力。

听说活动 3：通过图片激活学生关于公园景物的图式，学生根据自己的生活经验，描述公园中常见的景物。图片能给学生一定的提示，引导学生从动物、植物、人物、景物等方面进行描述。

二年级主题 6 Happy Holidays

听力材料

1.

Bill: Happy New Year! Where are you going?

Lily: Happy New Year! I am going home.

Bill: Me too!

2.

Chinese New Year is coming. People travel back to their home.

Bill: Families are having a reunion dinner. There is a lot of delicious homemade food.

Lily: I am so happy. I like egg rolls, noodles and shrimp.

Bill: Egg rolls symbolize wealth, because they are golden.

Lily: "Chang Ming" noodles shouldn't be cut, because long noodles symbolize health for a long life.

Bill: Shrimp symbolizes happiness, because shrimp sounds like smile.

3.

Bill: Hooray! I would get lucky money.

Lily: Why is it put in the red envelope?

Bill: In China, the color red symbolizes luck!

4.

Grandfather: This is for you! Best of luck!

Bill: Thank you! Grandpa. Wish you good luck.

5.

Lily: Look! Fireworks are lighting up the sky.

Bill: Wow! Dragon dancers are parading through the streets.

Lily: I like the red lanterns hanging in the street.

Mother: Yes, they are glowing in the night to bring good fortune to all.

6.

Families: Happy Chinese New Year!

Bill: Hope it all goes well this year!

听说活动

1.T: Listen and choose.

(1) What the topic is? (　　)

A. Chinese New Year　　B. National Day　　C. Christmas

Listen to the second dialogue and answer the questions:

(2) Why is everyone going home? (　　)

A. Chinese New Year is coming.　　B. They want to go home.

C. They will have a reunion dinner.

(3) How many kinds of food can you hear? What are they?

(4) Listen again and number the pictures:

( )   ( )   ( )

(5) Listen and match the special meaning of the food. ( )

A.wealth   B. happiness   C. health for a long life

2. Listen and answer.

(1) How many activities can you hear in this passage? ( )

A. two   B. three   C. four   D. five

(2) T: Why do people put the lucky money in the red envelope? What does the color red mean? Can you find the key sentence?

3. Listen and fill in the blanks.

①

②

③

④

4. T: Listen's recall.

(1) Can you say more food with special meanings?

(2) Why is the Chinese New Year important for us?

(3) Can you share about your memory of Chinese New Year?

课程设计者：珠海市斗门区齐正小学 华曼彤

本课内容选取了西方的重要节日——圣诞节，听力课程意在选取中国最重要的节日——春节，作为拓展。其中，春节的风俗和习惯学生都非常熟悉，听力文本内容贴近生活，容易勾起学生的回忆和兴趣。用英文介绍熟悉的中国节日，唤起学生对春节的美好回忆，激发学生的学习兴趣。

文本创设了多个双人对话，聊到春节特色食物的特征和寓意，以及过春节的风俗收红包、放鞭炮、舞龙等，以此展开听说学习。在听说训练中，听取细节信息，有利于锻炼学生的逻辑性思维，提高他们的语言知识和听说能力。

听力输入的新知结合中国传统文化知识背景，学生在此过程中可以进行深刻的思考、总结和表达，进而整合语言知识和语言技能，提高概括能力，达到深度学习的目的。

二年级主题 7 Playtime

听力材料

Miss Liu: Hello, Danica.

Danica: Hi, Miss Liu.

Miss Liu: Where are you going?

Danica: I am going to the park with my family.

Miss Liu: What can you do there?

Danica: I can **swim**, **play football** and **ride a bike**.

Miss Liu: Great! **Doing more exercise** is good for you. Oh, there is a river in the park. Can you **swim** in the river?

Danica: No, I can't. But I can **swim** in the swimming pool in the park.

Miss Liu: You are right. Can you **ride a bike**?

Danica: Yes. I can **ride a bike** with my mother.

Miss Liu: OK, have fun!

Danica: Thank you, Miss Liu. Goodbye!

Miss Liu: Goodbye!

听说活动

1. Listen and choose.

Miss Liu: Where are you going?

Danica: I am going to the park with my family.

(1) Where is Danica going? She is going to the ______________. (　　)

A.

B.

Miss Liu: What can you do there?

Danica: I can swim, play football and ride a bike.

What can Danica do? She can ________________________. (　　)

A.

B.

C.

D.

E.

2. Listen and circle.

Miss Liu: Great! Doing more exercise is good for you. Oh, there is a river in the park. Can you swim in the river?

Danica: No, I can't. But I can swim in the swimming pool in the park.

(1) Is there a river in the park?　(Yes, there is. / No, there isn't.)

(2) Can Danica swim in the river?　(Yes, She can. / No, She can't.)

(3) Where can Danica swim?　She can swim in the (river / swimming pool).

3. Listen and answer.

Miss Liu: You are right. Can you ride a bike?

Danica: Yes. I can ride a bike with my mother.

Miss Liu: OK, have fun!

Danica: Thank you, Miss Liu. Goodbye!

Miss Liu: Goodbye!

(1) Can Danica ride a bike in the park? (　　)

A. Yes, she can.　　　　B. No, she can't.

(2) Danica rides a bike with her __________. (　　)

A. mother　　　　B. father

4. Let's say.

What can you do after school? Discuss it with your classmates.

For example: I can make a model plane after school.

课程设计者：珠海市香洲区第十二小学 刘冰玉

本课的内容选取了西方的重要节日——圣诞节，听力课程意在选取中国最重要的节日——春节，作为拓展。其中，春节的风俗和习惯学生都非常熟悉，听力文本内容贴近生活，容易勾起学生的回忆和兴趣。用英文介绍熟悉的中国节日，唤起学生对春节的美好回忆，走进生活，激发学生的学习兴趣。

文本主要创设了多个双人对话，聊到春节特色食物的特征和寓意，以及过春节学生熟悉的风俗收红包、放鞭炮、舞龙等，以此展开听说学习。在听说训练中，听取细节线索，锻炼思维推理能力，有利于培养学生的逻辑性思维，使学生的语言知识学习和听说能力都能得到提高。

听力输入的新知结合中国传统文化知识背景，让学生在此过程中一次次进行深刻的思考、总结和表达。整合语言知识和语言技能，提高学生的思维概括能力，达到深度学习的目的。

二年级主题 8 Weather

听力材料

Good morning! This is a **weather** report. It's **windy** and **cold** in Zhuhai. You can fly a kite in the park. It's **sunny** and **hot** in Hainan. You can swim and play football. In Shanghai, it's **rainy** and **windy**. Please remember to take your umbrella. How about Beijing? Oh, it's **snowy** and **cold**! You can make a snowman now. That's all for today's **weather** report. Goodbye!

听说活动

1. Listen and choose.

Good morning! This is a weather report. It's windy and cold in Zhuhai. You can fly a kite in the park.

(1) What's the weather like in Zhuhai? (　　)

A. 　　B. 

(2) What can you do in the park in Zhuhai now? (　　)

A. 　　B. 

2. Listen and circle.

It's sunny and hot in Hainan. You can swim and play football. In Shanghai, it's rainy and windy. Please remember to take your umbrella.

(1) It's sunny and _______ (cool hot) in Hainan.

(2) It's rainy and cold in Shanghai. (Yes No)

3. Listen and answer.

Good morning! This is a weather report. It's windy and cold in Zhuhai. You can fly a kite in the park. It's sunny and hot in Hainan. You can swim and play football. In Shanghai, it's rainy and windy. Please remember to take your umbrella. How about Beijing? Oh, it's snowy and cold! You can make a snowman now. That's all for today's weather report. Goodbye!

(1) What's the topic (话题) of this passage? (   )

A. fly a kite   B. weather

(2) It's rainy and windy in Shanghai. You should take __________. (   )

A. a ruler   B. an umbrella

(3) Where can you make a snowman now? (   )

A. In Zhuhai.   B. In Shanghai.   C. In Beijing.

4. Speaking.

Find a weather report, and talk about it with your classmates.

For example: This is a weather report. It's sunny in Guangzhou.

课程设计者：珠海市香洲区第十二小学 刘冰玉

小学二年级学生应达到的听说技能，要求能够根据听到的语句识别图片。而本听说材料是一份天气预报，是对课本中天气主题的一个拓展，使二年级的学生能够在基本掌握描述天气的对话能力的基础上，还能独立完成播报天气的任务。4 个听说活动层层递进，对学生的听说能力提出更高的要求，使其最终实现深度学习的目标。

听说活动 1：是对文本的浅层分析，学生从听力材料中可以获取基本信息：某地的天气，以及在这个天气状况下我们可以从事的活动。

听说活动 2：难度增加，对学生捕捉细节、提取关键信息的能力提出了要求。同时通过听说活动，使学生掌握“在同一时间点，全国各地的天气各不相同”这一基本常识。

听说活动 3：难度继续加大。考查学生全面分析语篇的能力，如听力材料的主题是什么；考查学生判断能力，如在珠海、上海和北京三地，哪里可以堆雪人。

口语活动 4：通过学生对听力材料的认知加工，将知识转化成自己的文本输出。他们可以做一个天气预报，播报天气情况，最终达到深度学习的目的。

二年级主题 9　Seasons

听力材料

听力活动 1

Lily: Hello, Billy. Where are you?

Billy: I am in Beijing.

Lily: What's the weather like in **spring** in Beijing?

Billy: It is windy and warm. I can ride a bike.

听力活动 2

Lily: What's the weather like in **summer** in Beijing?

Billy: It is hot. I can swim.

Lily: What's the weather like in **autumn** in Beijing?

Billy: It is cool and dry. I can fly a kite.

Lily: What's the weather like in **winter** in Beijing?

Billy: It is cold. I can make a snowman.

听力活动 3

Lily: Can you make a snowman in **winter** in Zhuhai?

Billy: No, I can't.

Lily: What's the weather like in **winter** in Zhuhai ?

Billy: It is warm.

听说活动

1. Listen and circle.

听力材料

Lily: Hello, Billy. Where are you?

Billy: I am in Beijing.

Lily: What's the weather like in spring in Beijing?

Billy: It is windy and warm. I can ride a bike.

(1) Where is Billy?

A. In Zhuhai.

B. In Beijing.

(2) What is the weather like in spring in Beijing?

2. Listen and circle.

听力材料

Lily: What's the weather like in summer in Beijing ?

Billy: It is hot. I can swim.

Lily: What's the weather like in autumn in Beijing?

Billy: It is cool and dry. I can fly a kite.

Lily: What's the weather like in winter in Beijing?

Billy: It is cold. I can make a snowman.

(1) What's the weather like in summer in Beijing?

(2) What's the weather like in autumn in Beijing?

(3) What's the weather like in winter in Beijing?

3. Listen and answer.

听力材料

Lily: Hello, Billy. Where are you?

Billy: I am in Beijing.

Lily: What's the weather like in spring in Beijing?

Billy: It is windy and warm. I can ride a bike.

Lily: What's the weather like in summer in Beijing ?

Billy: It is hot. I can swim.

Lily: What's the weather like in autumn in Beijing?

Billy: It is cool and dry. I can fly a kite.

Lily: What's the weather like in winter in Beijing?

Billy: It is cold. I can make a snowman.

Lily: Can you make a snowman in winter in Zhuhai?

Billy: No, I can't.

Lily: What's the weather like in winter in Zhuhai?

Billy: It is warm.

(1) Billy can____________ in spring. (　　)

A. fly a kite　　B. ride a bike

(2) Billy can ___________ in winter.

A. swim　　B. make a snowman

(3) They are talking about___________ .

A. seasons　　B. time　　C. numbers

4. Retell and act in group.

(老师准备一些图片，如 swim, make a snowman, fly a kite, ride a bike。学生看着图片复述对话中的人物行为，并让学生演出来。)

5. Let's say.

What's the weather like in Hainan in winter? What can you do?

课程设计者：珠海市香洲区第十二小学 郭海茵

在日常生活中，四季的天气变化同学们都有体会。听力文本结合季节与中国的地方气候特点，用英语整合编排，再配上清晰简明的图画，考查了学生的信息处理能力。同时，本单元练习将我国其他地区四季的天气与珠海的天气相结合，能够引起学生的共鸣，给学生创造话题，激发学生的学习积极性。

创编文本融合了前面二年级主题 7 和主题 8 中关于基本活动和天气介绍的知识点，以课本的基础知识为蓝本展开听说练习，侧重培养学生的英语学科素养。在听说过程中，学生尝试捕捉听力材料中的有效信息，结合自己的生活经验，加以推理，锻炼了逻辑思维能力。

二年级主题 10 Times

听力材料

听力活动 1

Mr. Wolf is playing games with some animals.

Birds: Mr. Wolf, Mr. Wolf. What time is it now?

Mr. Wolf: It's 7:30. It is playtime.

Birds: Let's play!

听力活动 2

Dogs: Mr. Wolf, Mr. Wolf. What time is it now?

Mr. Wolf: It is 3:13. It's time to ride a bike.

Dogs: Let's go!

Cats: Mr. Wolf, Mr. Wolf. What time is it now?

Mr. Wolf: It is 4:40. It's time to swim.

Ducks: Let's swim!

听力活动 3

Cats: Mr. Wolf, Mr. Wolf. What time is it now?

Mr. Wolf: It is 5:50. It's time to fly a kite.

Cats: Let's fly a kite!

Rabbits: Mr. Wolf, Mr. Wolf. What time is it now?

Mr. Wolf: It is 12 o'clock. Let's have lunch!

Rabbits: Oh! Let's run!

听说活动

1. Listen and choose.

听力材料

Mr. Wolf is playing games with some animals.

Birds: Mr. Wolf, Mr. Wolf. What time is it now?

Mr. Wolf: It's 7:30. It is playtime.

Birds: Let's play!

(1) What are they doing? (　　)

A. They are playing games.

B. They are playing soccer.

(2) What time is it now? (　　)

A. 7:30

B. 8:30

2. Let's act.

听力材料

Dogs: Mr. Wolf, Mr. Wolf. What time is it now?

Mr. Wolf: It is 3:13. It's time to ride a bike.

Dogs: Let's go!

Cats: Mr. Wolf, Mr. Wolf. What time is it now?

Mr. Wolf: It is 4:40. It's time to swim.

Ducks: Let's swim!

Cats: Mr. Wolf, Mr. Wolf. What time is it now?

Mr. Wolf: It is 5:50. It's time to fly a kite.

Cats: Let's fly a kite!

Rabbits: Mr. Wolf, Mr. Wolf. What time is it now?

Mr. Wolf: It is 12 o'clock. Let's have lunch!

Rabbits: Oh! Let's run!

(1) Let's ride a bike. What time is it now?

(2) Let's swim. What time is it now?

(老师演示 ride a bike, swim, have lunch 等动作，学生回答时间。)

3. Let's retell.

(老师准备一些图片，如 swim, make a snowman, fly a kite, ride a bike 等。学生看着图片复述对话中的人物行为，并表演出来。)

4. Let's play.

Let's play games together.

课程设计者：珠海市香洲区第十二小学 郭海茵

《老狼老狼几点钟》这个游戏同学们都很熟悉。游戏化的句型训练，可以激发学生学习的积极性和自信心。相信通过这个游戏，学生可以更好地学习时间的问答。

创编文本融合了前面的主题 7 关于基本活动的话题。利用学生已学过的活动单词创编听说游戏剧本，从学生的最近发展区出发，融合传统游戏。在听说过程中，学生尝试捕捉听力文本中的有效信息，并做出基本的反映，最大化的将语言能力的学习和听说能力的学习融合。在多次反复过程中，学生要有意识地去模仿句型，重建信息，然后进行二次表达归纳，从而提升英语语言能力。

二年级主题 11 My Day

听力材料

Hello, my name is Yang Qian. I am studying in Tsinghua University. I am also a shooting player. I get up at 6:30. I **have breakfast** at 7:00. I go to school at 7:40. I **have lunch** at 11:50. I **go home** at 5:30. I **have dinner** at 6:00. I **go to bed** at 9:30. I like sports. I **do a lot of exercise** every day. I won the gold medal at the games of the Tokyo olympics. Do you like sports?

听说活动

1. Listen and choose.

(1) Who is a shooting player? (　　)

A. Ma Long　　B. Yang Qian　　C. Quan Hongchan

(2) Yang Qian is studying in________. (　　)

A. Peking University　　B. Tsinghua University　　C. The University of HK

(3) Yang Qian won the gold medal at the games of the__Olympic.

A. Tokyo　　B. Beijing　　C. London

2. Listen and number.

6 : 30

(　　)

7 : 40

(　　)

9 : 30

(　　)

7 : 00

(　　)

3. Answer.

(1) Do you like sports?

(2) When do you get up every day?

(3) When do you have breakfast every day?

(4) How do you go to school every day?

(5) When do you go home every day?

(6) When do you have dinner every day?

(7) When do you go to bed every day?

课程设计者：珠海市香洲区第十九小学 徐影

文章描述了奥运冠军杨倩的日常生活。通过听说练习，学生可以掌握时间的表达方法，同时了解相关的文化常识。在问答中，学生通过体验和探究，发现语言规律，逐步掌握语言知识和技能，形成有效的学习方法，提高自主学习能力。

听说活动 1：听短文选择正确答案。在学习英语的过程中，学生接触和了解文化常识，有益于对英语的理解和使用，有益于加深对中华传统文化的认识和热爱，有益于接受先进文化的熏陶，有益于培养国际意识。听力短文内容涉及文化常识，与学生的学习和生活密切相关，能激发学生学习英语的兴趣，提高学生对中外文化异同的敏感度和鉴别能力，进而提升交际能力。

问题（1）谁是射击运动员？选项当中出现三个学生熟知的奥运冠军，分别是马龙、杨倩和全红婵。通过听短文，学生可以选出正确答案，并积累奥运常识。

问题（2）杨倩是哪所学校的学生？选项当中出现三所著名的大学，分别是北京大学、清华大学和香港大学。通过听短文及从图片中提取信息，学生可以选出正确答案，并积累高校常识。

问题（3）杨倩获得了哪届奥运会金牌？选项当中出现三个举办过奥运会的城市，分别是东京、北京和伦敦。通过听短文，学生可以选出正确答案，并积累奥运常识。

听说活动 2：听短文给图片排序。学生在听完短文后，需要归纳主题并留意相关信息。在这个过程中，孩子们的听力技巧以及梳理和归纳能力得到有效训练。

听说活动 3：回答问题。听力短文为学生提供了句型示范，降低了表达难度，学生可根据实际情况，尽情描述自己每天做的事情。在学习过程中，学生乐于模仿，敢于表达，对英语具有一定的感知能力。这个过程锻炼了学生的口语表达能力和综合运用知识的能力。

二年级主题 12 My Week

听力材料

1. Jack: Ben, look! This is a timetable I made.

   Ben: Wow, so nice! What day is it?

   Jack: It's **Sunday.** Let's go to the park.

   Ben: OK!

2. Ben: What day is it?

   Jack: Let me see. Em... It's **Monday.**

   Ben: Oh, we are late! Let's go to school.

   Jack:OK!

3. Ben: Jack, what day is it ?

   Jack: It's **Wednesday**. It's Mum's birthday.

   Ben: Let's buy a birthday cake. What time is it?

   Jack : It's 5:30 p.m. Let's go.

4. Ben: Jack, it's **Friday**. Let's get up and go to school .

   Jack: No, it's **Saturday**. We don't go to school today.

   Ben: Hooray! Let's go out and play.

   Jack: OK! Let's go!

听说活动

1. Listen and choose.

Jack: Ben, look! This is a timetable I made.

Ben: Wow, so nice! What day is it ?

Jack: It's Sunday. Let's go to the park.

Ben: OK!

(1) What day is it today? (　　)

A. Monday　　B. Friday　　C. Sunday

Ben: Jack, what day is it ?

Jack: It's Wednesday. It's Mum's birthday.

Ben: Let's buy a birthday cake. What time is it?

Jack : It's 5:30 p.m. Let's go.

(2) What time is it? (　　)

A. 3:30 p.m.　　B. 5:00 p.m.　　C. 5:30 p.m.

2. Listen and circle.

Ben: What day is it ?

Jack: Let me see. Em... It's Monday.

Ben: Oh, we are late! Let's go to school.

Jack :OK!

(1) What day is it ? It's Sunday/Monday.

(2) We are late! Let's go to school/park.

3. Listen and answer.

Ben: Jack, what day is it ?

Jack: It's Wednesday. It's Mum's birthday.

Ben: Let's buy a birthday cake. What time is it?

Jack: It's 5:30 p.m. Let's go.

(1) It's Wednesday. It's ______ birthday. (   )

A. Dad's B. Mum's C. Jack's

(2) It's .Mum's birthday . Let's buy a ______. (   )

A. cake B. book C. ruler

4. Talk about the timetable with your classmates.

Example: It's Monday. Let's go to school.

TIMETABLE

Monday	Tuesday	Wednesday	Thursday	Friday	Saturday	Sunday
go to school	fly a kite	go to supermarket	play football	ride a bike	go swimming	sing a song

课程设计者：珠海市保税区第一小学 郝磊

以上的听力材料设计本意是通过 Jack 制作的 timetable 引入孩子日常情境。小学生在新学期都会制作 timetable，通过看制作的 timetable，学生可以知道哪一天做什么事情，从而培养时间规划能力。

听说活动 1：确定话题是由 timetable 带出。让学生思考日期问题时，可以通过看 timetable 得到答案；而问题（1）可以让学生学会思考如何回答“今天是星期几”这个问题，达到复习星期的相关单词的目的，进而完成第一阶段的学习目标。

听说活动 2：进一步练习回答“今天是星期几”这个问题。通过回答，引出周一是上学日的答案，进一步引发学生思考上学日和周末分别应该做什么事情。学生们在回答问题的同时，也认识到上学日是需要上学的这一观点，进而，达成了第二阶段的学习目标。

听说活动 3：引入情境纪念日，练习回答“今天是星期几”这个问题的同时，引导学生思考“今天是妈妈的生日，我们要做什么”的问题。第二个问题问几点钟，让学生认识到在适当的时间做适当的事情。练习强调了妈妈生日让学生明白要懂得感恩的道理，进而达成第三阶段的学习目标 。

听说活动 4：通过问“是否是周几”，练习回答是与否，引发学生思考一周当中每天需要做什么事情，不需要做什么事情。学生从问答问题到自己表述，达成第四阶段的学习目标。

三年级主题 1　Myself

听力材料

1. I am Joy. I am 9 years old. I'm in Class 2, Grade 3. I like reading and writing. One day, two friends from the *Big Tree School* wrote me two letters. It's a big surprise.

2. Dear Joy,

My name is Jack. I am a student from *Big Tree School.* I am ten years old. I'm in Class 3, Grade 4. In my school, there is a big tree. It's cool in summer. I can read under the tree. Do you like reading? I want to share my books with you. Let's be friends!

Yours,

Jack

3. Dear Joy,

I'm Lily. I'm a student from Xinjiang, *Big Tree School*. I am eight years old. I'm in Class 4, Grade 1. My friends and I like singing and dancing around a big tree. We can play under the tree. We read under the tree. But I don't know many words. Can you help me?

Yours,

Lily

听说活动

1. Listen and choose. (part 1)

(1) How old is Joy? (　　)

A. nine　B. eight　C. ten

(2) Which class is Joy in? (　　)

A. 2　B. 3　C. 4

(3) What does Joy like? (　　)

A. Joy likes reading and writing.

B. Joy likes singing and dancing.

C. Joy likes swimming.

2. Listen and choose. (part 2)

(1) Who writes the letter? (　　)

A.

B.

C.

(2) Which is the Big Tree School? (　　)

A.

B.

(3) Does Jack like reading? Do you like reading? Why?

教师可以先给出范例，I like reading. Because I like the pictures in the book. 引导学生用 Because 来回答，启发学生深入思考问题，刺激深度学习的发生。

3. Listen and answer.

(1) Where is the *Big Tree School*?

(2) Who are they? (Say their names)

(　　　)　　　(　　　)　　　(　　　)

(3) What do they like doing around the tree?

(4) Lily has some problems. Can you help her? How?

教师可以适当用中文进行引导，并引导学生用 I can... 的句型进行回答。允许学生在表达时个别语言使用中文，然后教师帮助学生组织语言，进行英文表述。该部分意在刺激学生思考和总结学习方法，并且善于帮助和引导他人学习的能力。

课程设计者：珠海市香洲区凤凰小学　于红蕾

《大青树下的小学》是部编版三年级语文上册第一单元的课文。本段听说材料以大青树下的小学为背景，结合课本中的书信交友方式，在语文和英语学科共同搭建的情境下，更能使学生投入其中。在文本的帮助下，学生除了能够掌握基础句型进行自我介绍外，也能通过书信中的文字描述锻炼抽象思维能力。文本将文字可视化、信息集中化，在提高学生整合能力的同时，也能发展学生的共情能力，让他们学会了了解关心他人，并且积极地付诸行动，从而促进学生的多元能力发展。

创编文本以书信为载体，包含了自我介绍中的基本语句结构和相关词汇输入，与本单元重点句型对应。听说活动注重语言的运用和输出，同时也强调学生情感的发展。

三年级主题 2 My Body

听力材料

The Tadpoles Look for Their Mommy

（英文版《小蝌蚪找妈妈》）

One day, the tadpoles wake up!

Tadpoles: Where is our mummy? Mummy, mummy, where are you?

A duck is coming.

Tadpoles: Mummy, mummy, I love you.

Duck: I' m not your mummy. Your mummy has **two big eyes** and **a big mouth**.

Tadpoles: Oh, thank you, see you!

*A fish is coming. It has **two big eyes** and **a big mouth**.*

Tadpoles: Mummy, mummy, I love you.

Fish: I' m not your mummy. Your mummy has **four legs**.

Tadpoles: Oh, thank you, see you!

*A tortoise is coming. It has **two big eyes**, **a big mouth** and **four legs**.*

Tadpoles: Mummy, mummy, I love you.

Tortoise: I' m not your mummy. Your mummy is green and white. She can swim and sing.

A frog is coming. It has ***two big eyes, a big mouth*** *and* ***four legs****. And it is green and white. It can swim and sing.*

Frog: Baby, baby, come here!

Tadpoles: Mummy, mummy, I love you .

听说活动

1. What is the topic of the passage? (　　)

A.　　　　B.　　　　C.

2. How do you know about them? What key words did you hear?

3. Listen and number.

(　　)　　(　　)　　(　　)　　(　　)

4. Let's retell.

duck→fish→tortoise→frog. (two big eyes, a big mouth and four legs, green and white)

课程设计者：珠海市横琴新区第一小学 刘小青

《小蝌蚪找妈妈》是一篇科学童话故事，学生非常熟悉，这有助于他们理解英文故事。听力文本根据中文故事改编，相似的句子反复出现，结构简单，朗朗上口，富有童趣，能提升学生的阅读兴趣。配上生动的插图，勾起学生对中文故事的回顾，激发学生自主阅读的内驱力。

结合主题My Body，学习巩固并拓展身体部位的单词。听说训练过程中，让学生关注细节，提取有用信息。同时注重完整的听力材料输入，触发学生对语篇思考的连续性，有利于培养学生的逻辑思维能力，提升他的语言知识运用能力和听说能力。

三年级主题 3　Food

听力材料

1.

Bill: Good morning, Yaoyao.

Yaoyao: Good morning, Bill.

Bill: I'm hungry. Do you want to have breakfast?

Yaoyao: Yes I do. I want an **egg**, some **bread** and **tomatoes** for breakfast.

Bill: Me too.

Yaoyao: And I want to have lunch with Lily.

Bill: That's nice. What do you want for lunch?

Yaoyao: I want some **chicken**.

Bill: What about dinner? Do you go home for dinner?

Yaoyao: Yes. I want some **vegetables** and **eggs**.

2.

Binbin: Hello, Joy!

Joy: Hi, Binbin.

Binbin: It's time for lunch. What food do you like for lunch?

Joy: I like **fish** and **noodles**. Do you like **fish**?

Binbin: No, I don’t. But I like **rice**. I want some **rice** and **meat** for lunch.

Joy: I want to go to the supermarket and buy some **food** for dinner.

Binbin: What do you want to buy?

Joy: I want to buy some **chicken** and **vegetables**.

听说活动

1. Listen to the first text.

(1) Listen and choose.

What do Bill and Yaoyao want for breakfast? (　　)

A.

B.

C.

(2) Listen again, fill in the blanks and read the sentences.

Bill: Good morning, Yaoyao.

Yaoyao: Good morning, Bill.

Bill: I’m hungry. Do you want to eat breakfast?

Yaoyao: Yes I do. I want an ______, some bread and ______ for breakfast.

Bill: Me too.

Yaoyao: And I want to eat lunch with Lily.

Bill: That’s nice. What do you want for lunch?

Yaoyao: I want some ______.

Bill: What about dinner? Do you go home for dinner?

Yaoyao: Yes. I want some _______ and eggs.

2. Listen to the second text.

(1) Listen and write down True (T) or False (F).

① Joy likes fish and noodles for lunch. (　)

② Binbin wants some rice and meat for lunch. (　)

③ Binbin wants to go to the supermarket. (　)

(2) Role play with your partners to talk about the food you want for lunch.

教师可以先找学生示范，并给出范例，-Hello, Joy! What do you want for lunch? -I want some meat and rice.

(3) Listen again, read and draw the food that Joy wants to buy.

Joy: I want to go to the supermarket and buy some food for dinner.

Binbin: What do you want to buy?

Joy: I want to buy some chicken and vegetables.

Joy wants to buy ...

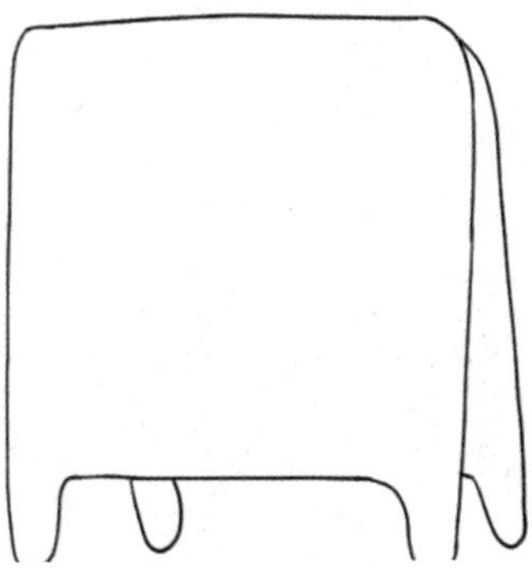

课程设计者：珠海市高新区金凤小学 张驰

《英语课程标准》(2011 年版)强调在语境中理解语言，体会并归纳语言的用法，根据特定的语言需求，运用语言进行交流。

听说活动 1：通过 Dad，Lily 和 Mom 的交流可知，他们想去超市购买食材。家庭成员们先是表达自己想吃的食物，并在 Mom 的带领下列出购物清单。这个情境联系学生的实际生活，激活了他们的背景知识，学生能提取有效信息并进行归纳总结。

听说活动 2：发生在日常生活交往中，Joy 向 Andy 表明她肚子饿了想要吃午饭，Andy 回应并表示出想要一起去吃午饭的意愿。学生能根据 hungry，lunch 等关键词，确定情境发生的时间及他们交流的目的，准确梳理信息。

三年级主题 4　Pets

听力材料

1.

Hello, I'm Lily. This is my **pet**. I love it very much. It's a **chicken**. It's yellow. It has two small eyes and two legs. Do you have a **pet**? Can you tell something about your **pet**?

2.

Joy: Wow! What a beautiful **dog**!

Yaoyao: Thank you. Do you have a **dog**?

Joy: No, I don't. But I have a **cat**.

Yaoyao: What does it look like?

Joy: It has two big eyes. And it has a small body and a long tail. I love my **cat**.

听说活动

1. Listen to the first text.

(1) Listen and tick.

Hello, I'm Lily. This is my pet. I love it very much. It's a (chicken / duck).

It's (orange / yellow). It has two (small / big) eyes and two (legs / feet). Do you have a pet? Can you tell something about your pet?

(2) Listen and choose.

① Does Lily love her pet? (　　)

A. Yes, she does.　B. No, she doesn't.

② Guess! What else (其他的) does Lily's pet have? (　　)

A. Lily's pet has wings.　B. Lily's pet has hands.

2. Listen to the second text.

(1) Listen, choose and fill in the blanks about Joy's cat. Share them with your partners.

Joy's cat has two ______(big / small) ______(ears / eyes). And it has a ______(big / small) ______(tail / body) and a ______(long / short) ______ (tail / body).

(2) Pair work: Listen again, tell your partners the key words you heard. And draw Joy's pet together.

课程设计者：珠海市高新区金凤小学 张驰

《英语课程标准》要求教师充分利用自身的生活经历与经验以及学生的学习经验和实例，丰富教学内容。本单元内容 Pets 贴近学生生活，引导学生关注人与宠物。

听说活动 1：通过 pet，chicken，dog，cat 等关键词，学生能推理归纳出文本描述的内容与宠物的特征有关，教师可引导学生根据已有的经验提取并概括相关信息。

听说活动 2：通过日常交流展开。Joy 碰见了 Yaoyao，并对 Joy 的宠物猫进行了赞美，从而展开了有关养宠物的话题。话题贴近学生生活，学生能根据已有经验进行判断，并在梳理文本的同时关注细节信息。

三年级主题 5 Clothes

听力材料

It's winter. It's a cold and snowy night. A cute little girl is walking with no **shoes** in the street. Her feet are red and blue. And she is hungry. She wants to eat bread and meat. She lights up a match. It's warm. This is a magic fire! She sees her grandma. Grandmother says: "Wear your **coat** and **shoes**. It's cold outside." Then she sees her mother. Her mother says: "Sweetie, wear your red **gloves** and **cap**. It's winter."

听说活动

1. Listen and choose.

Which season is it? (　　)

A. Winter

B. Spring

C. Summer

D. Autumn

2. Listen and answer.

(1) What's the weather like?

(2) What does her grandmother say? (　　)

A. wear a sweater

B. wear a coat

C. wear a jacket

D.wear a scarf

(3) What does her mother say? (　　)

A. wear gloves

B.wear shoes

C. wear trousers

D. wear a dress

3. Lets' say.

(1) What should the little girl wear?

(2) What do you wear in winter?

课程设计者：珠海市高新区金凤小学 杨淑瑜

听力文本结合本单元主题和安徒生童话故事，通过改编《卖火柴的小女孩》，创设语言情境，激发学生兴趣。文本语言难度适中，与学生已学知识相关，可以培养学生跨文化交际意识。

创编文本结合三年级学生已学知识，包括颜色、食物、家庭人物和季节、天气，以安徒生童话故事为蓝本，凸显跨文化学科素养。听说练习题结合不同题型，层层递进，激活学生迁移运用的思维。

三年级学生知识储备有限，听说活动设计借助童话故事和丰富的图片降低了听力难度。部分听力文本内容以图片形式展示，学生需要进一步结合图片理解听力内容。学生在这个过程中，锻炼了理解、辨别、运用知识的能力。

三年级主题 6 Birthday

听力材料

Hello, my name is Minmin. I'm eight years old. My birthday is coming. Do you know when it is? Yes, it's on the Chinese New Year. It is known as Spring Festival. It is usually in January or February. Before Spring Festival, people clean rooms and buy new clothes. On that day, my family and friends often say "Happy New Year" and "Happy Birthday" to me. We eat Jiaozi and noodles together. It's fun.

When is your birthday? Share with me!

听说活动

1. Listen and choose. When is Minmin's birthday? (　　)

A. Christmas

B. Spring Festival

C. Mid-Autumn Festival

2. How old is Minmin in the coming (即将到来的) Spring Festival? What key words did you hear?

3. What people do before Spring Festival? (　　)

A. clean rooms

B. buy fruit

C. buy clothes

D. play football

4. Please draw what Minmin and her friends eat on her birthday.

5. Listen and read the story. Share your birthday to your classmates.

(1) When is your birthday?

(2) What do you do on your birthday?

课程设计者：珠海市高新区金凤小学 杨淑瑜

听力文本结合本单元主题和中国传统节日，通过中国女孩讲述生日及传统节日活动，创设语言情境，激起学生兴趣。文本编排合理有趣，贴近学生生活，蕴含中国文化知识，培养学生跨文化交际意识。

创编文本结合前几个主题的知识点，包括年龄、食物和衣服主题，融入劳动教育，凸显学科素养和育人观念。听说练习题结合不同题型，层层递进，激活学生思维，让他们学会迁移运用知识。

三年级学生知识储备有限，听说活动设计借助丰富的图片降低听力难度，把听力文本内容以图片形式展示。学生需要结合图片理解听力内容。这个过程锻炼学生理解、辨别、迁移知识的能力。

三年级主题 7 My School Subjects

听力材料

Andy Tiger likes sports very much. Today is his first day in Happy Animal School. He is so excited and happy. Look! His teacher is coming! She is Ms. Sheep.

Ms. Sheep: Welcome to the school! I am Ms. Sheep.

Andy Tiger: Hello, Ms. Sheep. I am Andy Tiger.

Ms. Sheep: Hi, Andy Tiger. Do you like our school?

Andy Tiger: Yes, I do. What classes do we have in a week, Ms. Sheep?

Ms. Sheep: We have **Chinese**, **maths**, **English**, **science**, **art**, **music,** **computer** class and **PE** in a week. We can read poems in Chinese class, play games in English class and look for the rule of numbers in math class.

Andy Tiger: What can we do in other classes?

Ms. Sheep: We can do experiments in science class, sing and dance in music class, draw in art class and write programs in computer class.

Andy Tiger: What about PE?

Ms. Sheep: You can do exercise in PE class.

Andy Tiger: Wow, I like doing exercise. I will be an athlete in the future. I love PE!

Ms. Sheep: I believe you will make it. Today is Monday. Andy, we have **Chinese**, **English** and **maths** on Monday.

Andy Tiger: Oh, do we have **PE** on Monday?

Ms. Sheep: Sorry, no.

Andy Tiger: Oh, no. Let me have a look. We have **science**, **computer** class, **Chinese** on Tuesday. And on Wednesday, we have **art**, **music** and **PE**. What classes do we have on Thursday, Ms. Sheep?

Ms. Sheep: We have **English**, **art** and **PE** on Thursday.

Andy Tiger: How about Friday?

Ms. Sheep: We have **maths**, **music** and **science** on Friday. Andy, do you like these classes?

Andy Tiger: Yes... But if...

Ms. Sheep: What do you want?

Andy Tiger: I want to have **PE** every day!

Ms. Sheep: Aha, my dear, Please put up your hands. Look, there are ten fingers on your hands. Every subject is like a finger. Every finger is important. Do you want to lose any fingers?

Andy Tiger: No! I will enjoy all of them.

听说活动

1.Listen to the dialogue and circle the answers.

听力材料

Andy Tiger likes sports very much. Today is his first day in Happy Animal School. He is so excited and happy. Look! His teacher is coming! She is Ms.

Sheep.

(1) Who are they? They are ______. (　　) (多选题)

A. 
B. 
C. 
D. 

(2) Where are they? They are in the _________. (　　)

A. 
B. 

C. 

2. Listen and number.

听力材料

Ms. Sheep: Welcome to the school! I am Ms. Sheep.

Andy Tiger: Hello, Ms. Sheep. I am Andy Tiger.

Ms. Sheep: Hi, Andy Tiger! Do you like our school?

Andy Tiger: Yes, I do. What classes do we have in a week, Ms. Sheep?

Ms. Sheep: We have Chinese, maths, English, science, art, music, computer class and PE in a week. We can read poems in Chinese class, play games in English class and look for the rule of numbers in math class.

Andy Tiger: What can we do in other classes?

Ms. Sheep: We can do experiments in science class, sing and dance in music class, draw in art class and write programs in computer class.

Andy Tiger: What about PE?

Ms. Sheep: You can do exercise in PE class.

(　　)　　(　　)　　(　　)　　(　　)

(　　)　　(　　)　　(　　)　　(　　)

3. Listen and put the words into right places. Find out on what day they have these classes.

听力材料

Ms. Sheep: I believe you will make it. Today is Monday. Andy, we have Chinese, English and maths on Monday.

Andy Tiger: Oh, do we have PE on Monday?

Ms. Sheep: Sorry, no.

Andy Tiger: Oh, no. Let me have a look. We have science, computer class, Chinese on Tuesday. And on Wednesday, we have art, music and PE. What classes do we have on Thursday, Ms. Sheep?

Ms. Black: We have English, art and PE on Thursday.

Andy Tiger: How about Friday?

Ms. Sheep: We have maths, music and science on Friday. Andy, do you like the classes?

Andy Tiger: Yes..., But if...

Ms. Sheep: What do you want?

Andy Tiger: I want to have PE every class every day!

Ms. Sheep: Aha, my dear, Please put up your hands. Look, there are ten fingers on your hands. Every subject is like a finger. Every finger is important. Do you want to lose any fingers?

Andy Tiger: No! I will enjoy all of them.

Word Bank:

Monday Tuesday Wednesday Thursday Friday Chinese

PE English art music maths

Day	Classes		
	Chinese	English	
	science	computer class	
	maths		science
	art		music
			PE

4. Let's say.

Listen again and answer the questions:

(1) What do you learn from the story?

(2) If you were Andy, what will you say at last?

(3) How will you make your favorite timetable at school?

课程设计者：珠海市金湾区航空新城小学 李迎紫

听说活动 1：通过听故事的前情提要，指明对话的人物是小老虎和羊老师。随后通过第二个问题，让孩子思考对话发生的地点。孩子通过小老虎是新同学这一信息，推理出他们对话发生在学校，并根据从已有经验中提取相关信息。这可以锻炼他们的思维。

听说活动 2：通过听对话，看图，标序号。孩子们从小老虎和羊老师的对话中，了解了学校有什么课程，学生能在课程中做什么活动。在标序号的过程中，孩子们捕获细节信息的能力得到锻炼，提高了听认技巧。

听说活动 3：让孩子听小老虎和羊老师的最后一段对话，内容主要为讨论一周课程的安排。学生将得到一个信封，把听到的单词选出来，补全表格，通过听力回归主题。在这个过程中，孩子们的综合听力能力、梳理归纳能力得到有效提高。

口语活动 4：通过让孩子再次听一遍完整的故事，回答开放式问题，给他们提供了自由发挥的空间。孩子们可根据自己的认知理解，利用本单元的目标语言、句型，给出答案。既可谈谈自己对故事的理解，设身处地为主角着想，又可围绕单元主题设置自己喜欢的课程表，将学到的知识运用到实际生活中。

三年级主题 8　My School

听力材料

Welcome to Red Star No.1 Primary School. Our school building is very big. It has three floors .

We have a **science room**, an **art room** and **a library** on the first floor. We can do some experiments (做实验) in the **science room**. We can draw beautiful pictures in the **art room**. We can read books in the **library**.

We have some **classrooms** and two **toilets** on the second floor. We can study in the classroom. We can wash our dirty hands in the **toilet**.

We have a **teachers' room** , a **computer room** and a **music room** on the third floor. We can sing and dance in the **music room**.

We also have a big **playground**. We can play football and games. We love our school.

听说活动

1.T: Listen to the first paragraph and guess what the topic is.（　　）

A. A classroom

B. A school

C. A library

2. T: Let's listen to the whole passage and stick(粘贴) the pictures in the blanks.

The third floor			
The second floor			
The first floor			

附：参考答案

The third floor			

The second floor			
The first floor			

教师给学生提供单元重点词汇图片，学生在听语篇的过程中，两人合作完成*Building Designer*活动——把文本中提到的功能室贴在相应楼层。根据图片和关键词，引导学生能用 We have a ... 的句型简单说出教学楼的设计。该活动旨在提升学生的理解能力和概括能力。

1. T: Listen to the whole passage and match.

( )	( )	( )

( )	( )	( )

A. We can sing and dance.

B. We can read books.

C. We can play football and games.

D. We can study a lot.

E. We can draw beautiful pictures.

F. We can do experiments.

5. Let’s say.

Do you like your school? Can you introduce it?

课程设计者：珠海市横琴第一小学 陈洁

通过本单元的学习，学生能够利用重点词汇和句型来描述学校教室、场馆、功能室及其楼层位置。话题与学生的校园生活息息相关，能够引起学生的学习兴趣。听力文本整合改编了课内知识，拓展了功能室的用途。学生以校园小导游的形式，介绍教学楼的设计，以它为底本展开听说学习，难度稍微高于学生的语言水平，但是均为可理解性的语言材料。听说过程中，教师不仅要引导孩子学会从语篇中抓住关键词，获取关键信息，还要从整体上理解语篇信息，获取大意。通过完整的听力输入，培养学生的逻辑思维能力和语言知识的运用能力。

通过一定量的听力输入和形式丰富的活动，学生可以更好地理解吸收学习内容，并通过实践和口头输出，掌握和内化所学知识。

三年级主题9 After School Activities

听力材料

A little monkey lives in a forest with his parents and friends. His name is Sammy.

Sammy: I'm going to be the best monkey in this forest. You will know my name!

Mommy monkey: My dear boy. To be the best monkey, you need to learn lots of things. That's very hard for a young monkey like you.

Sammy: I'm not afraid. Just wait and see.

One day, Sammy sees a little bird flying through the sky.

Sammy: Hey, little Bird! What are you going to do?

Little Bird: I'm going to find the tallest tree in the forest. And I'm going to stand at the top of that tree! Wind! I can feel the wind!

Sammy: Wow. That's a good way to prove I'm the best monkey. I'm going to learn how to climb trees!

When Sammy is heading to find the tallest tree in the forest, he sees a little bear standing near the river.

Sammy: What are you going to do?

Little Bear: I'm going to catch the biggest fish in this river.

Sammy: Wow. That's amazing. I'm going to learn how to catch fish, too!

Suddenly, a little tiger runs past Sammy.

Sammy: Hey, Tiger! Why are you in such a hurry! What are you going to do?

Little Tiger: I'm going to race with the rabbit. I'm going to be the fastest runner in the forest!

Sammy: Wow! That's a good idea. I'm going to learn how to run faster, too.

Three months later, Sammy's mother sees Sammy sitting under a big tree, crying sadly.

Mommy Monkey: What happened, my child?

Sammy: I don't know what I'm going to do. I want to learn how to climb trees, how to catch fish, how to run faster. But I don't have time to do so many things together. I can't be the best monkey forever!

听说活动

T: Let's listen to the story together. Can you guess who is the main character in the story? (　　)

A. 

B. 

C. 

D. 

T: Let's listen to the story again. Try to complete the chart in time order.

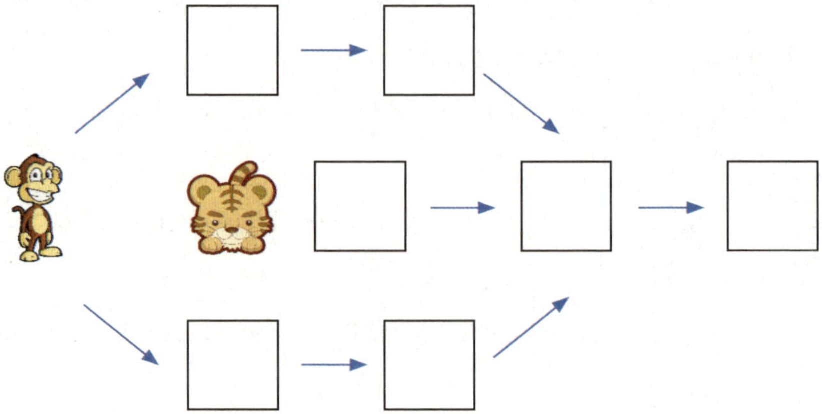

A.  B.  C. 

D.  E.  F. 

T: Please number the sentences in right order.

( ) A. Sammy is crying sadly under a big tree.

( ) B. Sammy is going to learn how to climb trees.

( ) C. Sammy is going to learn how to catch fish.

( ) D. Sammy wants to be the best monkey in the forest.

( ) E. Sammy is going to learn how to run faster.

T: We are going to listen to the story one more time. After listening, please try to answer the questions below.

1. How many things does Sammy want to learn?

2. Are these things suitable(适合) for Sammy?

3. Do you think Sammy can be the best monkey in the forest? Why?

T: If you are Sammy's mother, what will you say to Sammy?

Below are some phrases or sentences that might be helpful:

Don't be sad.

You just need to focus on learning one thing first.

In my heart, you are already the best monkey in the forest.

Be brave.

课程设计者：珠海市横琴第一小学　陈洁

在本课的学习中，学生将初步接触一般将来时 be going to do 句型。本听说材料通过小猴子 Sammy 想要成为最厉害的猴子的故事，带领孩子们反复操练新授句型。该听说练习以生动活泼的小故事为内容载体，通过画故事框架图、句子排序、回答问题以及自编结局等丰富多彩的练习形式，增强学生的逻辑推理能力与信息整合能力。

听说活动 1：要求孩子们在第一次听材料的过程中，根据故事内容推断故事主角，从整体上把握听力内容，激活孩子们头脑中对过往知识的印象，为接下来的精听环节做好准备。

听说活动 2：要求孩子们在第二遍听力结束后，完成故事框架图。在第二遍听材料的过程中，学生需要对整个故事的前后逻辑进行梳理，这需要学生在充分理解听力内容的基础上，对故事发生的时间顺序与主角行为的逻辑进行合理推理与排序，以完成此项任务。本活动的设计旨在加强学生对关键信息的抓取能力与逻辑推理能力。

听说活动3：需要学生按照故事发生的时间顺序，对重点句子进行排序。本听说活动中的句型基本为听力文本中重点操练的be going to do句型，设计的主要目的是让学生在听说活动的过程中，将注意力放在重点句型的辨认上，从而达到对重要知识点认知与理解的目的。

听说活动4：要求学生在第三遍精听的基础上，回答三个问题。想要回答这三个问题，仅复述文本当中的具体细节是行不通的。学生需要在充分理解文本内容的基础上，添加自己对于文本内容的理解与看法，才能完整回答问题。本听说活动的设计目的在于锻炼学生的语言组织能力与思辨能力。

听说活动5：要求学生为文本材料编写一小段结尾。通过完成此前的四个听说活动，学生对故事内容已经有了充分的认知与判断。听说活动5需要学生带入猴子妈妈的角色，思考小猴子最后什么都学不会的原因，最终编一小段猴子妈妈可能会说的话。每个孩子对于这个故事的感受都可能不同，有些孩子可能会说一下勉励小猴子的话，有些孩子可能会安慰小猴子，最终故事的结局由孩子们根据自己对故事的理解决定。此外，该活动对于基础较弱的孩子存在一定难度，教师可为此类孩子提供单词、短语或句型上的参考文本，帮助孩子顺利完成听说活动。

三年级主题 10 Hat

听力材料

Suzy Pig: Oh, a hat! I wonder whose hat is it.

Hello, tiger! Is this your hat?

Tiger: No, it isn't. My hat is brown.

Suzy Pig: Hi, monkey! Is this your hat?

Monkey: No, it isn't. My hat is not yellow. It's pink.

Suzy Pig: Hello, duck! Is this your hat?

Duck: No, it isn't. My hat has a big beautiful bow on it.

Suzy Pig: Hello, sheep! Is this your hat?

Sheep: I'm sorry. It's not my hat. My hat is tall.

Suzy Pig: Hello, Miss cat! Is this your hat?

Miss Cat: Yes, it is! This is my hat! My hat is small. My hat is yellow. My hat has two long ears, too! Thank you, Suzy Pig!

Suzy Pig: You are welcome, my dear!

听说活动

T: How many animals are there in the story? (   )

A. five   B. six   C. four   D. seven

T: We are going to listen to the dialogue for the second time. After listening, please match the hats with their owners.

A.    

B.    

C.    

D.    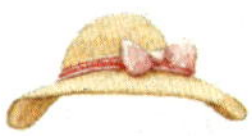

T: We are going to listen to the dialogue for the third time. Please circle the adjectives you hear in the conversation.

hat   big   tall   black   brown   short   cold   pink
small   yellow   pig   not   am   long   bow   monkey
sheep   my   your   tiger   pig   beautiful   hot

T: Can you draw Miss Cat's hat?

T: Maybe you also have a hat. Can you draw your hat and introduce your hat to the class?

(Miss Cat: My hat is small. My hat is yellow. My hat has two long ears, too!)

课程设计者：珠海市金湾区航空新城小学 谢梦如

在本单元中，学生重点学习了be动词引导的一般疑问句的构成与使用。本听力材料通过小猪Suzy找帽子主人的故事，反复加强学生对be动词引导的一般疑问句的熟悉程度。在寻找帽子主人的过程中，每个小动物都提到了自己的帽子的关键特征，这一类信息的训练能够加强学生的整合与推理能力。最后的两个听说活动在锻炼学生的信息整合能力的同时，也能够充分发挥他们的创造能力。

听说活动1：通过对听力文本中对话角色数量的提问，让学生在第一遍泛听中，将注意力放在对话的大致主题与参与对话的主要角色上。通过增强学生对文本大意的初步把握，让学生对接下来的精听环节做好准备。

听说活动2：是一道连线题，要求学生将帽子的主人与帽子相连。听力材料中，每个小动物都有提及自己帽子的显著特征，比如big，small，pink，tall等。学生在听的过程中，需要通过抓取关键形容词，并加以推理，才能顺利完成听说活动2。

听说活动3：要求学生挑选出听到的所有形容词。在本课中，学生要学会使用简单的形容词描述人或物的特征。本听说活动通过对形容词、名词、代词等各词性之间的对比与辨析，帮助学生加强对形容词的认知与理解，同时训练他们在听说活动中抓取关键信息的能力。

听说活动 4：要求学生通过对听力信息的整合与分析，推理出 Miss Cat 的帽子款式。该听说活动更注重学生对整体内容的理解与把握。学生在理解听力内容的基础上，要据小动物们的描述进行推理与整合，以精准地还原帽子的样式。与单纯让学生复述描写帽子的语句相比，绘画的形式更加有趣，也更能发挥学生的创造能力。学生可以在还原帽子关键特征的基础上充分发挥自己的想象力，画出又各具特色的帽子。

口语活动 5：要求孩子介绍自己的帽子。为了消除孩子们开口说英语的恐惧心理，本活动让学生将自己的帽子画下来，先为学生提供一个具体的描述对象。此外，在进行活动时，教师也可以呈现听力材料中 Miss Cat 描述帽子的语句以及其他可用于描述帽子的形容词，为学生提供句型与词汇上的参考，帮基础较弱的学生搭好脚手架，消除他们的恐惧，最终顺利进行表达。

三年级主题 11　Family Activities

听力材料

Family Pig are living in a small village. One day, Daddy Pig and Mummy Pig are going to **visit relatives** in the town. Three pigs want to go with them. They come to Aunt Tina's home.

Three Pigs: Hello, Aunt Tina. What are you doing?

Aunt Tina: I am **cooking dinner**.

Three Pigs can't see Uncle Paul. Then they ask Aunt Tina.

Three Pigs: What is Uncle Paul doing?

Aunt Tina: He's **watering the flowers** near the lake.

Three Pigs **go to the lake** and **water the flowers** with Uncle Paul. After a while, they want to **play with their cousins**, May and John. Then they ask Uncle Paul.

Three Pigs: What are May and John doing?

Uncle Paul: They are having fun. May is **flying a kite.** John is **playing his toys**.

Three Pigs **go to the garden** first. They **fly kites** with May. They have lots of fun. In one hour, they go back to the house. John isn't in his room. Where is he? They are looking for him.

Three Pigs: John, John! Where are you? What are you doing?

A voice comes out from Aunt Tina's room.

John: Shh! I am here. The room is full of toys. It's messy now. My mom will very angry at me. So I am **cleaning the room**.

Three Pigs: Take it easy. Let us help you!

Then May comes and joins them. Now they are all **sweeping the floor**!

听说活动

1. T: Listen to the story. Choose the main characters of the story. (　　)

A. Aunt Tina　B. Uncle Paul

C. Three Pigs　D. Cousin May　E. Cousin John

2. T: Let's listen to the story again. Try to number the picture in the right order.

A. 

B. 

C. 

D. 

E. . F. 

3. T: Please judge the sentences. If it's right, write "T"; if it's wrong, write "F".

Three Pigs go to Aunt Tina's home with friends.( )

Aunt Tina is feeding the fish.( )

Uncle Paul is watering the flowers.( )

May is riding a bike in the garden.( )

Three pigs help John clean the room finally(最后).( )

4. T: We are going to listen to the story one more time. After listening, please fill in the blanks and try to retell the story.

One day, Pig Family pay a visit to their relatives. Aunt Tina is________________________. Uncle Paul is _________________. May is flying a kite in the garden. John is ________________ in his room. But John makes the room messy. Now he is _____________ with three pigs. Then May joins them. They are helpful. What a happy day!

5. T: If you are Aunt Tina, what will you say to Three Pigs or May? What will you say to Paul?

What will Aunt Tina do to praise（奖励）them?

课程设计者：珠海市金湾区航空新城小学　郭晓丹

在本课的学习中，学生将初步接触现在进行时 be doing 句型。本听说材料通过 Family Pig 去亲戚家做客，以三只小猪（Three pigs）寻找不同的人分别在干什么，带领孩子们反复操练新授句型。该听说练习以 Aunt Tina 亲戚家为内容载体，通过初步概括主要人物、故事图片排序、判断句子对错、填空复述故事以及猜测故事结局等丰富多彩的练习形式，增强学生的逻辑推理能力与信息整合能力。

听说活动 1：要求孩子们在第一次听材料的过程中，根据故事内容推断故事主角，从整体上把握听力内容，激活孩子们头脑中对过往知识的印象，为接下来的精听环节做好准备。

听说活动 2：要求孩子们在第二遍听力结束后，对故事图片进行排序。在第二遍听材料的过程中，学生需要捕捉整个故事的关键信息，并对故事的前后逻辑进行梳理。这需要学生在整体把握故事的基础上，对故事发生的时间顺序与主角行为的逻辑进行合理推理与排序。本活动的设计旨在加强学生的关键信息抓取能力与逻辑推理能力。

听说活动 3：需要学生根据听说活动 2，参照图片及听力内容，对重点信息进行判读。本听说活动中的句型基本为听力文本中重点操练的 be doing 句型，设计的主要目的是让学生在听说活动的过程中，注重对目标句型的辨认与解读。

听说活动 4：要求学生在第三遍精听的基础上，完成短文的填空，并且将故事完整复述出来。在听的过程中，孩子们需要及时将关键信息记录在横线上，再次操练了 be doing 句型，巩固了新学的知识。本听说活动的设计目的在于锻炼学生抓取关键词的能力以及书写速度。

听说活动 5：要求学生回答故事结尾的几个发散性问题。通过完成此前的四个听说活动，学生对故事内容已经有了充分的认知与判断。听说活动 5 需要学生带入猪阿姨 Aunt Tina 的角色，换位思考，引发他们对猪弟弟 Paul 爱乱扔玩具的坏习惯的思考，检讨自己在生活中是否有此类行为。对于助人为乐的三只小猪及猪妹妹 May，猪阿姨 Aunt Tina 是怎么夸奖和奖励他们的，孩子们也能畅所欲言，联系生活实际，将其迁移至具体情景中。本听说活动的设计目的在于发散学生的思维。

三年级主题 12 My Home

听力材料

Little Tom is a naughty dog. Everyone in Joy's family knows that. He likes playing hide–and–seek everywhere. Sometimes he makes some troubles.

It's a nice day. Joy's family are busy at home. They are having a cleaning day. Joy is sweeping the floor in the room. But, where is Little Tom?

Joy: Where's Little Tom, Mom?

Mom: He's in the **kitchen**. He's drinking some water.

But Little Tom isn't there. The **kitchen** is messy now.

Joy: Where's Little Tom, Dad?

Dad: He's in the **garden**. He's playing a ball.

But Little Tom isn't there. The **garden** is messy now.

Joy: Where's Little Tom, grandma?

Grandma: He's in your **bedroom**. He's sleeping in the bed.

But Little Tom isn't there. The **bedroom** is messy now.

Joy: Oh, no! He makes a mess! Grandpa, where's Little Tom?

Grandpa: He's in the **living room**. He's watching TV.

But Little Tom isn't there. The **living room** is messy now.

Joy: Little Tom, where are you?

Oh, he is in the bathroom. He's taking a shower.

Everywhere in the house is messy. But Little Tom is clean now!

听说活动

1\. T: Which places does Little Tom go? ______________________

Please write the letters in the blanks.

A. bedroom B. living room C. dining room

D. study E. kitchen F. garden G. bathroom

2\. T: We are going to listen to the dialogue for the second time. After listening, please match the activities with the places.

A.  

B.  

C.  

D.  

E.  

3. T: We are going to listen to the dialogue for the third time. Please number the sentences in the right order.

( ) Joy's family are busy at home.

( ) The bedroom is messy now.

( ) He's in the garden. He's playing a ball.

( ) Little Tom is a naughty dog.

( ) He is in the bathroom. He's taking a shower.

( ) He's in the living room. He's watching TV.

4. T: Which title do you like best? Why? (   )

A. A Naughty Dog

B. Little Tom Makes A Mess

C. Cleaning Day?

5. T: If Little Tom wants to help them clean up the house, guess where he is and what he is doing. Draw a picture and try to introduce it.

(Example: Little Tom is washing his toys in the bathroom.)

课程设计者：珠海市金湾区航空新城小学　郭晓丹

本单元重点学习了 be 动词 + 地点的构成与使用。本听力材料通过家庭清洁日，Joy 寻找淘气小狗 Little Tom 的故事，反复加强学生对 Where 引导的特殊疑问句的提问以及 be 动词 + 地点的回答的使用。在寻找小狗 Little Tom 的过程中，Joy 的家庭成员都提到了他的位置以及正在进行的活动，这类信息的训练能够加强学生对信息的整理与归纳能力。最后的两个听说活动在锻炼学生的信息整理与归纳能力的同时，也能够充分发挥他们的想象力与创造力。

听说活动 1：通过对听力文本中出现的地点场景的考查，让学生在第一遍泛听中，将注意力集中在故事主线上。通过增强学生对故事大意的理解，让学生为接下来的匹配图片环节做准备。

听说活动 2：是一道连线题，要求学生将故事场所与对应的活动相连。听力材料中，每一个地方小狗都经过了并且有“捣乱”的行为。学生在听的过程中，需要通过抓取关键形容词，并加以推理，才能顺利完成听说活动 2。

听说活动 3：要求学生在第三遍听力过程中，对文本中出现关键信息的句子进行排序。在主题 11 和 12 中，学生需掌握现在进行时以及对地点位置的描述。本听说活动通过前面对文章脉络的大致梳理，加深了学生对情节的印象，使他们进一步从文章细节中把握文本。

听说活动 4：要求学生通过对文本的整体把握，给文章选择合适的标题，并说明原因。该活动锻炼了学生的高阶思维，教师应尽可能让学生用英文去表达自己的见解。教师可以给学生搭建好脚手架，举例说明其中的一个题目，引导学生自主思考，提升创新能力。

口语活动 5：要求学生发挥想象力，描绘出小狗帮忙清洁屋子的情景，并加以介绍。为了消除学生们开口说英语的恐惧，本活动让学生将小狗帮忙做家务所进行的活动与场所画下来，先在纸上为孩子提供一个具体的描述对象，以免学生们无物可以参考。

四年级主题 1 Sports and Games

听力材料

Hello, my name is Peter. I am 10 years old. I am in grade 4 at No.1 Primary School. I like sports. My favourite sport is **playing ping-pong**. I am good at it. I often **play ping-pong** with Andy and Bill on weekends.

My friends like doing different things on their weekends. They like outdoor activities. Susan likes **playing basketball**. Tim likes **going roller skating**. Coco likes **running** with her father. Joy likes **jumping rope**. She's good at **jumping rope**. We all like having fun on weekends.

听说活动

1. Listen again and number the pictures in right order.

		1		

2. Listen to the passage and match the pictures.

Susan　　Coco　　Peter　　Tim　　Joy

3. Talk to your partner about what she/he likes to do on weekends.

What do you like to do on weekends?

I like going roller skating. I am good at it.

4. Talk about you and your friends' weekends.

Hello, I am …

I often …

I am good at...

This is my friend...

She / He often …on weekends.

课程设计者：珠海市斗门区实验小学　蒋锦红

本文通过Peter介绍周末活动引出话题。语篇结合本单元所学“Sports and Games”的主要内容，融合三年级相关的知识，丰富语言基础，降低听说的难度，激发学生交流的兴趣。

听说活动的设计体现了层次性和指向性。语篇的内容在书本知识的基础上进行推进，达到复习旧知，巩固新知的目的。

听说活动1和2：先让学生看图片然后再听短文，学生抓住核心词汇进行输出，可以更好地理解和记忆短文的内容。这两个活动训练学生的图片记忆和理解能力。

听说活动3：学生通过前面的听力获取了更多的信息，教师创设合理的情景让学生进行交流，并正确运用核心词汇与句型对周末的活动进行问答和介绍，提升学生处理和加工信息的能力。

听说活动4：承接听说活动3的信息，老师引导学生模仿短文说说自己和朋友周末经常做的事情，让学生跳出文本，把所学的知识运用到现实生活中，加深学生对语言内容和语言学习过程的了解。

四年级主题 2 On the Weekend

听力材料

Mike: Hi, everyone. I'm Mike. The Sports Meeting is coming. Many students are practicing on the playground. Let's go and see. Look! Andy and Peter are **playing basketball**. Hello, Andy. You **play basketball** very well. Do you often **play basketball**?

Andy: Yes, I do. I often **play basketball** on the weekend. I'm good at **playing basketball**.

Mike: Good for you! What about you, Peter? What do you often do on the weekend?

Peter: I often **go fishing**, **climb a hill** or **play basketball**.

Mike: Very good! Wish you good luck in the Sports Meeting.

Mike: Hi, Bill. Do you want to **play basketball** with them?

Bill: No, I don't. I don't like outdoor activities.

Mike: What do you often do on the weekend?

Bill: I often **watch TV** on the weekend. Sometimes I **play computer games** all day.

Mike: That's not good for your eyes. Do more sports. Do you want to **play ping-pong** with me on the weekend?

Bill: Yes, I do.

Mike: Then see you on the weekend.

Bill: OK.

听说活动

1. Listen and choose.

(1) Who are playing basketball? (　　)

A. Mike and Andy　　B. Bill and Andy　　C. Andy and Peter

(2) Does Andy often play basketball on the weekend? (　　)

A. Yes, he does.　　B. No, he doesn't.　　C. I don't know.

(3) Who will play ping-pong on the weekend? (　　)

A. Mike and Andy　　B. Mike and Bill　　C. Andy and Peter

2. Listen and answer.

(1) What does Peter often do on the weekend? Is it good for him?

(2) What does Bill often do on the weekend? Is it good for him?

3. Listen and categorize, which activities are good and which are bad.

A. often play basketball	B. play computer games all day	
C. go fishing	D. climb a hill with friends	E. often watch TV
F. play ping-pong		

(1) Good: ________________________

(2) Bad: ________________________

4. Listen again and try to interview some of your friends.

课程设计者：珠海市斗门区实验小学　黄彩琴

听力文本让 Mike 以现场报道和采访形式出现。故事的情节是一位同学对几位即将参加运动会的运动员的采访，可以引发学生浓厚的学习兴趣。

文本主要以“On the Weekend”中所学知识，结合了几个不同主题的知识点，对学生进行多方面训练，突出学科语言和学科思维。听说训练过程中，听取细节线索，唤醒思维推理能力，同时也注重完整不间断的听力输入，触发了学生进行连续性的思考，有利于培养学生的逻辑性思维，提高学生的语言知识学习和听说能力。

学生用听力输入的语言回答问题，并且对相关知识进行分类。在这个过程中，学生需要一次次地深入思考、总结和表达，提升了思维和概括能力，达到了深度学习的目的。

四年级主题 3 Transportation

听力材料

Bill and Andy are from Beijing. Bill and Andy like Zhuhai very much. They are going to visit Zhuhai in winter holiday. They will come to Zhuhai **by plane**. On the first day, they are going to visit Zhuhai Museum **by bike**. Then they are going to Xiangshanhu Park **by bike**, too. On the second day, Bill and Andy are going to Doumen **by bus.** They will eat delicious food in Doumen. On the third day, they are going to Zhuhai Chimelong Ocean Kingdom **by taxi.** They will take many photos there! Then, they are going back to Beijing **by train**.

听说活动

1. T: Listen and number.

( )

( )

(　)

(　)

2. Listen and choose.

(1) Bill and Andy are from ___________. (　)

A. Guangzhou　B. Beijing　C. Zhuhai

(2) How are they going to Xiangshanhu Park? (　)

A. By bus.　B. By bike.　C. On foot.

(3) How are they going to Doumen? (　)

A. By bus.　B. By plane.　C. By train.

(4) How are they going back to Beijing? (　)

A. By ship.　B. By bus.　C. By train.

3. Listen and answer.

(1) How are they going to Zhuhai?

(2) What are they going to do in Doumen?

(3) Where are they going on the third day?

4. Can you retell the story by the mind map?

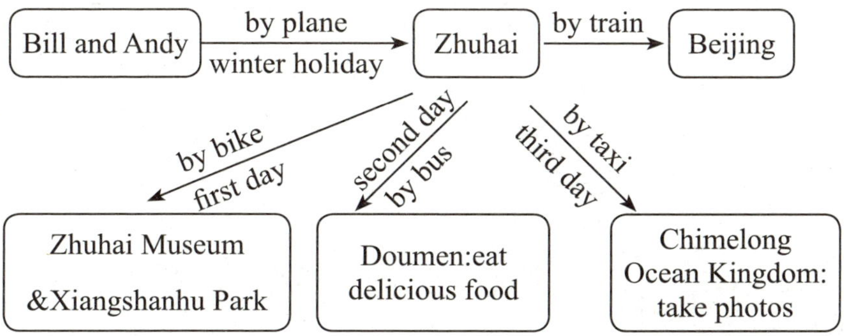

课程设计者：珠海市斗门区实验小学　陈素娜

文本结合本单元所学“交通工具”的内容，以珠海旅游线路为线索，贴近学生生活，可以引发学生浓厚的学习兴趣。

听说训练注重训练学生听取细节线索及整理信息的能力。

听说活动 1 和 2：和通过给图编号、选择等题目，帮助学生梳理故事细节，让他们在脑海中形成故事内容的框架；

口语活动 3：根据故事内容向学生提出三个问题，考查学生对故事内容的理解。在这一部分，学生根据听力过程中提取的细节信息，归纳故事内容并回答问题，听力技巧和归纳能力得到有效训练。

口语活动 4：学生通过前三个活动，基本理解和掌握故事大意，可以根据提示，复述这一故事。在实际练习中，基础好的学生可以脱离提示词，用自己的语言进行复述。在这两个口语活动中，学生需要用听力输入的语言和细节口头回答问题或复述故事情节。这需要学生进行进一步的思考、总结和表达，提升了学生的思维和概括能力。通过从听到说、由浅入深的活动训练，学生最终达到深度思考和学习的目的。

四年级主题 4　Asking for Help

听力材料

Lily, Ben and Tony are having art class. They are making cards for their teacher, Miss Wang.

Lily: I want to draw a yellow cat on the card. Ben, Can I use your yellow crayon, please?

Ben: Sure. Here you are.

Ben: I want to cut some birds for the card. Lily, can I use your scissors, please?

Lily: Sorry, I don't have scissors.

Ben: Tony, Can I use your scissors, please?

Tony: Sure. Here you are. Do you have a glue stick? I need to stick the flower on the card.

Ben: Sorry. I don't.

Lily: I have a glue stick. Here you are.

Tony: Thank you.

听说活动

1. Listen and circle.

They need...

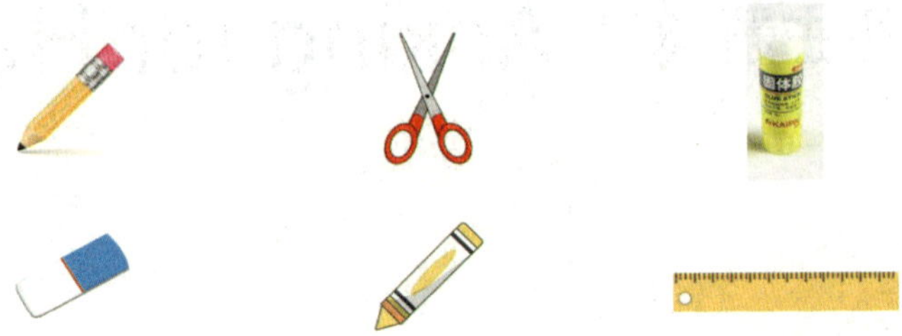

2. Listen and answer the questions.

(1) What are they doing in the art class?

(2) Does Lily have a glue stick?

(3) What does Ben want to cut?

3. Role play.

In the math class...

In the PE class...

In the science class...

In art class	In math class	In PE class
Do you have scissors?	Do you have a ruler?	Do you have a rope?
Can I use your glue stick?	Can I use your pen?	Can I use your ball?
Sure. Here you are.	Sure. Here you are.	Sure. Here you are.
Thank you.	Thank you.	Thank you.

课程设计者：珠海市斗门区实验小学　王亚雨沙

文本是一段孩子们上美术课的对话，结合本单元所学“Asking for help”

这一主题，学习一些关于文具的单词和寻求帮助的重要句型，同时对学生进行多方面的教育。对话的情节编排合理有趣，激发了学生浓厚的学习兴趣。

听说训练注重训练学生听取细节线索及整理信息的能力。

听说活动 1：由浅入深，第 1 题通过相关的图片，帮助学生边听边在脑海中形成对话内容的框架。

听说活动 2：根据对话内容向学生提出三个问题，考查学生对对话内容的理解。在这一部分，学生根据听力过程中提取的细节信息，归纳对话内容并回答问题，听力技巧和归纳理解能力得到有效训练。

口语活动 3：学生通过前 2 个活动，基本理解和掌握对话大意，可以结合课本主题，进行交际。通过思考不同场景中寻求帮助和提供帮助的使用语，提高学生在实际生活中应用英语的能力，并进行价值观教育，让学生明白寻求帮助的重要性，呼吁学生敢于表达，敢于寻求帮助。本材料通过从听到说、由浅入深的活动训练，使学生达到深度思考和学习的目的。

四年级主题 5 Safety

听力材料

Today is Monday. Peter, Sam and John are at school. Look, they are playing now. Peter is running down the stairs. Sam is climbing on the window ledge. John is playing basketball in the classroom. They are so happy but the teacher is very angry. She asks them to stop. It's very dangerous!

(The bell rings) It's time to go home. All of the children walk out of the school. Peter's home is far from the school. He always waits for his father at the school gate. Sam usually goes home on foot. Look, he is waiting for the green light. What about John? He is 12 years old. He can go home by bike.

听说活动

1. Listen and number.

( )

( )

( )

( )

( )

2. Listen and match.

Peter Sam John

3. Listen and categorize.

Safe:

Dangerous:

A. Climb on the window ledge

B. Run down the stairs

C. Wait for father at the school gate

D. Wait for the green light

E. Play basketball in the classroom

F. Go home by bike after 12 years old

4. Let's say.

For safety, what should we do and what shouldn't we do in the school and out of the school?

课程设计者：珠海市斗门区莲洲镇横山中心小学 杨结萍

本单元重点在于学习“为了确保安全，学生需要形成的好习惯及规则”。每个课时都有大量内容让学生学习，知识比较零散。而笔者设计了分场景的听说材料，根据校内与校外两个场景，大致把教材中的好习惯及规则进行了分类，能够帮助学生在脑海中形成知识架构，同时，拓展了学生日常学习生活中可能存在的不正确的行为，潜移默化地教育学生形成良好的行为习惯。

听说活动 1：让学生通过听录音排序，初步了解全文的大意，创造条件让他们思考与锻炼理解能力。学生通过了解大意，可以突破对细节的理解障碍，为下一步学习做好准备。

听说活动 2：让学生匹配姓名与相应的活动，有目的地听取细节信息，完善对文本的理解，锻炼其听取信息的能力。

听说活动 3：让学生听录音并且判断哪些学生的行为存在安全隐患。此活动不是简单的信息对应活动，需要学生具有一定的理解和判断能力，比之前的活动更具挑战性。

口语活动 4：通过让学生讨论在校内与校外应该如何确保安全，同时进行语言学习与安全教育。

四年级主题 6 Jobs

听力材料

Hello, boys and girls. I am Miss Li. Today we are going to talk about future **jobs**. Let's welcome Leo, Bella and Lydia to talk about their future **jobs**.

Hello, everyone. My name is Leo. I am twelve. I am in Class 2, Grade 6. I like cooking. I can cook. I am good at cooking. I always cook for my family. I want to be a **cook**. I like yummy food.

Hi, my name is Bella. I am ten. I am in Class 1, Grade 4. I am good at writing. But I don't want to be a **writer.** My favorite subject is art. I like painting. I want to be a **designer** in the future. I want to design some clothes. I like beautiful clothes.

Good morning, I am Lydia from Class 3, Grade 5. I am eleven. Do you like animals? I like animals very much. I like playing with dogs, cats, rabbits and so on. At weekends, I always help my aunt in the pet shop. I am happy to stay with animals. I want to be a **vet** in the future. I can take care of animals.

Thank Leo, Bella and Lydia for sharing their future jobs. What about you? What do you want to be in the future?

听说活动

1. Listen and choose.

(1) How many students are there in the sharing? (　　)

A. 2　　B. 3　　C. 4

(2) Who can cook well? (　　)

A. Leo　　B. Bella　　C. Lydia

(3) Bella is from ________________. (　　)

A. Class 2, Grade 6　　B. Class 1, Grade 4　　C. Class 3, Grade 5

(4) Does Bella want to be a writer? (　　)

A. Yes, she does.　　B. No, she doesn't.　　C. We don't know.

(5) What does Lydia like playing with? (　　)

A. animals　　B. toys　　C. Friends

2. Listen and match.

Leo

Bella

Lydia

3. Listen again and fill in the blanks.

Name	Good at	Want to be
Leo		
Bella		
Lydia		

4. Let's say.

(1) What are you good at?

(2) What do you want to be in the future?

课程设计者：珠海市斗门区莲洲镇横山中心小学　任思敏

本文主要内容为一名老师邀请了三位学生，与同学们展示自己的特长，以及自己的理想职业方向。故事主要以本单元所学"Jobs"为主题，并且结合主题 1 中 I like..., I am good at... 和 I can... 句型对学生进行多方面的训练。

听说训练，注重训练学生听取关键信息的能力。

听说活动 1 和 2：难度较低，是选择题和配对题，学生只要认真听，就可以得到大部分答案。选择题中，特意增加了有关数量的题目，主要是因为有些学生对数字不敏感。

听说活动 3：难度增加，学生除了要从对话中提取重要的信息，还要写出来。也许有很多单词他们不一定一听就能写出来，教师可以多播放几次，鼓励学生根据读音猜出单词，可以借助自然拼读的规则。

口语活动 4：是根据对话内容向学生提出的两个问题，学生可以通过两两对话、小组对话、个人汇报、小组汇报等方式，展示自己的特长以及对未来职业的憧憬。教师鼓励学生多角度思考职业的多样性，并以正能量加以引导，必要时可以增加一些与某种职业有关的感人事迹或趣闻来辅助教学。

四年级主题 7 My Neighbourhood

听力材料

I have a dog, Bobby. It is cute but very naughty. We live in a great Neighbourhood. Today I get up at 8:00. But Bobby is not at home. “Where is Bobby?”

First, I go to the park, because Bobby likes to play with balls in the park. But Bobby is not there. Then, I get to the school. The school is next to the park. But Bobby is not in the school.

There is a grocery across from the school. In the grocery, I meet my neighbor, Miss Lee. “You should go to the police,” Miss Lee says.

So, I go to the police office. I go straight and turn left at the first crossroads. I see a cinema on the left. Then, I keep walking. Finally, I see the police office is between the bookshop and the bank.

I talk to the police officer that I lost my dog, Bobby. The police officer asks, “Is it that white dog?” “WOOF, WOOF, WOOF!”.

听说活动

1. T: Listen to paragraph 1 and choose the title for the passage. (　　)

A. Where is My Dog?

B. My Dog—Bobby!

C. I Love My Neighborhood.

2. T: Listen to paragraph 2, 3, 4 & 5 and number the pictures.

(　)

(1)

(　)

(　)

(　)

(　)

3. Listen to the paragraph 5 and answer questions.

Question 1: Where is the dog?

Question 2: What does the dog look like?

4. T: Listen to the whole passage and complete the map.

A.

B.

C.

D.

5. T: Listen to the whole passage again and pick out the words you hear.

以小组为单位，分发信封。信封里装着本单元的重点单词和短语。学生将再一次听完整个语篇，并进行 Pick up the Words 的竞赛，将听到的单词挑出来，即听力文本中画线的单词。教师邀请学生把听到的关键词贴在社区地图的相应位置，建立起这则故事的思维导图，为接下来的“Design a neighbourhood tour”活动搭建支架。

6. T: Design a neighborhood tour and present your tour plan to the class.

通过前几个听力训练，学生已对这个社区的场所以及相应功能有了一定的了解，接下来学生将以小组为单位，设计“A Neighbourhood Tour”，向大家展示游玩线路、时间安排并解释设计原因。

课程设计者：珠海市高新区永丰小学　唐倩钰

从单元主题 My Neighbourhood 出发，以寻找宠物犬 Bobby 为线索，创编了“Where Is My Dog？”这则小故事。跟着主人寻找 Bobby 的线路，带领学生认识该社区。

创编听力文本融合了本单元的知识点，涵盖各场所的单词、方位词、问路的句型。在开展听力训练过程中，学生先听这则故事的首段，选择合适的标题。学生可根据文本中提及的背景信息，预测故事的发展，培养逻辑性思维能力。紧接着，学生将会跟着主人的脚步，开展寻找 Bobby 的旅途。在此过程中，学生需要听取细节线索，如寻狗的路线、社区各场所的具体方位，培养提取关键信息的能力。除了了解方位，通过听力文本的阅读，了解社区内各个场所的功能，从而让学生建立社区概念，并且为接下来的学习打下基础，建立大单元学习意识。

在听力输入完成后，学生以小组为单位，依托社区路线图和思维导图，设计并向大家介绍该社区的游玩线路，并解释这样设计的原因。这一过程中，学生将充分调动本单元学习到的语言知识和语言技能，锻炼时间规划以及合理安排的能力，由此完成目的语的输出以及认知能力的提高。通过“听”和“说”的有机结合，实现语言和综合能力的提升。

四年级主题 8 Cities

听力材料

Sue meets her new friend Mike in a new city ...

1.

Mike: Hello, Sue! Nice to meet you!

Sue: Hello, Mike! Nice to meet you, too!

Mike: Welcome to our city. I hope you will have a good time!

Sue: Thank you! I want to see a film first. How can I get there?

Mike: It's not far. We can walk there. Let's go!

2.

Mike: I like the film Harry Porter very much.

Sue: Me too! Is there a city museum? I want to see old things.

Mike: Yes. It's near the cinema. We can ride a bike there.

3.

Sue: It is a big and interesting city. Now I am hungry. I want to eat noodles. Where is the restaurant?

Mike: We can take a subway. It's between the bookshop and the post office.

Sue: Great! I can buy some books and postcards there.

4.

Sue: I need some new clothes. Let's go to the shopping mall. How can I get there?

Mike: It's far. Here is the bus station. We can take a bus.

Sue: Nice idea!

听说活动

1. Look and guess.

T: Weekend is coming. Sue comes to a new city. Where does she go? How does she go there? What's in the city?

2. Listen, read and say.

T: There are many fun places in the city. What are they? Let's find out.

(1) Sue wants to see a film there. What is it?

(2) Sue likes seeing the old things there. What is it?

(3) Sue wants to buy some books there. What is it?

(4) Sue is hungry. She wants to eat noodles. What is it?

(5) Sue wants to send postcards to her friends. What is it?

(6) Sue wants to go shopping and buy some clothes there. What is it?

3. Listen and choose.

T: Sue wants to go to different places. How can Sue get there? Let's listen and write.

A. take a bus	B. walk
C. ride a bike	D. take a subway

4. Look and say.

T: Sue has a good day. Let's talk about the city!

5.Let's recall the story.

The city is very interesting. There are many fun places in the city. There is a ____. We can see a film there. It's not far. We can _____ there. There is ___. We can see old things there. We can _____ there. There ________. It's between the _________. We can _____ there. We can ______there._________. _________. ______. I like the city.

6. Draw and write.

T: How about you? Where do you want to go? How do you get there? Please draw and write it down.

Sentence patterns: There is a ... in my city. It's across from / next to / between ... . I want to ... . I can ... .

7. Show time.

学习评价

My reflection 我的反思	
Listen carefully and try to take notes. 认真听录音，并尝试做笔记。	
Speak loudly. 大声说英语。	
Think actively and creatively when speaking and writing. 在完成说和写的任务时，积极思考，并发挥自己的创造力。	
Learn to summarize and review. 学会总结，并复习。	

课程设计者：珠海市三灶镇中心小学 何瑞妮

在主题7中，我们学习了如何在语境中用英语来描述城市中常见场所的词汇，以及所处的位置；本单元在主题7的基础上，训练学生在语境中学会询问去某地应乘坐何种交通工具。

通过听、读、说等方式，学生能够听懂询问去某地应乘坐何种交通工具的语篇，从中提取关键信息；借助地图完成选择交通工具的任务，描述城市中常见场所的词汇，以及所处的位置；了解、分析和描述人或事物的位置，以及根据实际情况选择乘坐的交通工具，并模仿语篇进行小创作。

四年级主题9 Travel Plans

听力材料

Summer holiday is coming. Tom and Lisa are happy, because they are going to travel with their parents in this summer holiday.

First, they want to go to **Hainan** by plane. They want to stay in a big hotel near the sea. They want to eat seafood. And Tom wants to swim in the sea. Lisa wants to play beach volleyball with their parents.

Next, they want to go to **Chengdu** by train. They want to see pandas in the zoo. And Tom wants to take photos with pandas. He likes them. Lisa wants to try the hot pot. It's yummy and spicy.

Finally, they want to take a high–speed train to **Beijing**. They want to visit the Great Wall. Tom wants to watch shows. Lisa wants to row a boat on the lake.

It's a nice travel plan. They will have fun in the trips.

听说活动

1. T: Listen to the first paragraph and guess what the topic is.

( ) A. The travel plan of summer holiday

( ) B. The travel plan of winter holiday

2. T: Number the pictures. Where do Tom's family want to go during this summer holiday?

( )

( )

( )

3. T: How do they go there? Match the pictures and the places.

Beijing Chengdu Hainan

4. T: Let's listen to the whole passage and judge.

( ) (1) They want to stay in a hotel on the mountain in Hainan.

( ) (2) They want to see tigers in Chengdu.

( ) (3) They want to visit the Great Wall in Beijing.

5. T: How do you know about them? What key words did you hear?

6. T: Listen to the whole passage again and discuss in groups to finish the form.

Places	**What does Tom want to do?**	**What does Lisa want to do?**
Hainan		
Chengdu		
Beijing		

7. T: Can you share your summer holiday plan? Please talk about your plan in your groups.

(1) Where do you want to go?

(2) Who do you want to go with?

(3) How do you want to get there?

(4) What do you want to do there?

课程设计者：珠海市三灶镇中心小学　龙婉婷

本听力文本结合了本单元知识重点，突出一般现在时的运用、乘坐交通工具的表达以及一般现在时主语为第三人称时动词的变化规则。文本以Tom、Lisa一家的暑假旅游计划为背景，计划去哪个城市旅游，乘坐的交通工具，结合当地的旅游景点、美食特色以及假期活动，为学生听说课程提供贴近生活的题材，让学生熟悉城市特点，激发学生学习的兴趣。同时学生在对前两个话题的学习与理解的基础上，综合运用之前学过的知识，更加灵活地运用语言。

听说活动 1：学生初次听，提取重要信息，思考并概括文本主旨大意。

听说活动 2 和 3：根据初步对文本信息的提取，抓住关键信息点，对 Tom 一家暑假旅游城市的顺序进行编排，训练学科思维能力。

听说活动 4：学生再听文本，并抓取细节信息，进行思考与判断，培养语言听说能力和思维能力。

听说活动 5 和 6：学生对文本主要信息进行整理归纳，培养分析和归纳总结能力。

听说活动 7："听"是对输入信息的"加工"，"说"是表达，是"输出"，没有输入就没有输出。在听懂的基础上说，增强说的能力，使两者有机结合，相互促进。模仿听力输入的语言，整合运用语言，养成用英语进行思考、听说、交流的学习习惯。学生听得投入，才有兴趣使用语言进行交流，才能体会学习英语的快乐。

四年级主题 10 Hobbies

听力材料

Hello, my name's Jack. I have three good friends: Lucy, Linda and Tim. They have different (不同的) **hobbies**.

Lucy is short but she's good at **playing basketball**. She often **plays basketball** with her classmates after school. She thinks it can make her strong and healthy.

Linda is a shy girl. **Reading** is her hobby. She reads many kinds of books, such as story books, novels and so on. She can get lots of knowledge from books.

Tim is a creative boy. When he was a little boy, he likes **model planes**. He saves his money to buy many kinds of model planes. He studies English hard for (为了) talking with foreign model lovers (外国模型爱好者).

Different people have different **hobbies**. So, what's your **hobby**? Why do you love it?

听说活动

Part 1: Listening.

1. Listen and choose.

听力材料：Hello, my name's Jack. I have three good friends: Lucy, Linda and Tim. They have different hobbies.

(1) Jack has ______ good friends. (　　)

A. 　　B. 　　C. 

(2) What's the topic (主题) about? (　　)

A.  hobby　　B.  animal

2. Listen and circle.

听力材料：Lucy is short but she's good at playing basketball. She often plays basketball with her classmates after school. She thinks it can make her strong and healthy.

(1) Lucy is ( short /  tall).

(2) Lucy's hobby is ( baseball /  basketball).

3. Listen and judge.

听力材料：Linda is a shy girl. Reading is her hobby. She reads many kinds of books, such as story books, novels and so on. She can get lots of knowledge from books.

(1) Linda is shy. (　　)

(2) Linda likes writing books. (　　)

4. Listen and fill in the blanks.

听力材料：Tim is a creative boy. When he was a little boy, he likes model planes. He saves his money to buy many kinds of model planes. He studies English hard for talking with foreign model lovers.

(1) Tim likes ___________ .

(2) He studies _________ hard.

Part 2: Speaking.

(1) What's your hobby?

(2) Why do you like it?

课程设计者：珠海市三灶镇中心小学　郭艳君

本单元谈论“爱好”这个话题，文中三个孩子有各自的爱好，有喜欢运动的，有喜欢看书的，有喜欢模型飞机的。听力材料从孩子们身边的朋友聊起，不仅可以让孩子产生强烈的共鸣，还能让他们学习“爱好”这一话题的语言表达方式。

文本第一段简明扼要地介绍自己和三位朋友，还表明三位朋友有不同的爱好，从而引起孩子往下读的兴趣。

文本第二段介绍了一位叫 Lucy 的女孩儿。她虽然个子不高，但是热爱打篮球。文本向学生暗示，热爱一件事情跟其他条件无关，以及热爱运动的好处。

第三段谈到了害羞的 Linda 喜欢阅读。表达“爱好”的句式以“Reading is her hobby.”方式呈现，使学生了解、掌握多种表达“爱好”的方式。学生通过理解文本还能认识到书本的种类，并明白“书中自有黄金屋”的道理。

第四段讲述了拼模型是很多孩子的爱好。听力材料以 Tim 这位孩子为例，讲述了他所遇到的两个困难，并通过存钱和努力学英语来坚持自己的爱好的故事。它告诉孩子们，热爱可能是短暂的，唯有坚持才能长久。

最后设置了两个口语活动，一是询问孩子们的兴趣爱好是什么；二是为什么喜欢这些爱好？听力材料从别人聊到自己，激起孩子“说”的欲望。这是两个开放性问题，没有标准答案，有利于孩子们自由表达。

四年级主题 11 Free Time

听力材料

Hello! My name is Linda. I'm from China. My favorite activity is swimming. I usually go swimming twice a week with my parents. Do you want to swim with me?

Hello! My name is Bob. I come from America. I like playing soccer. I often play soccer with my friends after school. We play soccer three times a week. It's a lot of fun!

Hello! I am Jack. I'm from Australia. I am good at playing the piano. I practice the piano everyday. Sometimes I play the piano with my friends. It's interesting!

听说活动

1. T: Listen to the passage and match. Where do they come from?

Linda **Bob** **Jack**

Australia **China** **America**

2. T: Listen to the passage and answer the questions.

(1) What does Linda like doing?

____

(2) What does Bob like doing?

____

(3) What is Jack good at?

____

3. T: How often do they do their favorite activities? Listen, write and draw.

(1) ________goes swimming ________.

(2) ________plays soccer ________.

(3) ________practices the piano ________.

4. Let's say.

Group work: What do you often do in your free time? Ask your friends and finish the form.

- What is your favorite activity?
- How often do you do it?

Name	**Favorite Activities**	**Frequency**

5. Speaking.

Can you talk about your favorite activities? And talk about your friends' favorite activities.

课程设计者：珠海市三灶镇中心小学 龙婉婷

本听力文本结合本单元知识重点，以来自三个不同国家的小朋友介绍自己的兴趣爱好为主线，结合一般现在时时态的运用以及活动频率的表达，为语言交流应用提供日常生活素材。它通过运用已有的语言知识逐步将学生的听说思维引向有序和深入，从而培养学生思维的系统性和深刻性。在 *My hobby* 的基础上，让学生认识到利用 *Free time* 进行自己喜欢的活动的重要性，最终实现前后单元的整合学习。

听说活动 1：学生初步认识三位小朋友，提取人物的基本信息。

听说活动 2：根据对三位小朋友的初步认识，了解个人兴趣爱好，然后对信息进行筛选和梳理，写下主要信息。

听说活动 3：学生再听文本，有侧重点地提取细节信息，对活动频率的表达进行思考，培养语言听说能力和思维能力。

听说活动 5 和 6：通过让学生对文本主要信息进行整理和归纳，培养学生分析和归纳、总结问题的能力。

听说活动 7：听是接受语言的表现，说则是思维表达的表现。这一进一出，是大脑与外界交流的基本表现形式。二者相辅相成，缺一不可。

四年级主题 12 Countries

听力材料

I am Jenny. I am a Chinese girl. I like traveling. You can visit the Great Wall of **China** in my country. And I like making friends, too. Look, they are my new friends. They are Andy, Alice, Harry and Joy.

Andy is an **American** boy. His favorite hobby is taking pictures. He can watch a parade and take some pictures with Micky Mouse in the Disneyland.

She is Alice. She comes from **France**. She likes making models. She can make a model of Eiffel Tower.

Harry likes drawing pictures. He's from **Canada**. He enjoys a lot of shows in a big circus park.

Singing and dancing are Joy's favorite hobbies. She is an **Australian** girl. She watches lots of music shows in the Sydney Opera House.

听说活动

1. T: Look, she is Jenny. Where is she from? What's her hobby? What can you do in her country?

2. T: Jenny wants to make new friends. Who are they? Choose one of

Jenny's friends and talk about it.

Eg: (1) Who is he/she? Where is he/she from? What's her/his hobby? What can you do in his/her country?

3. T: How many countries can you hear? What are they? Listen and choose.

(1) How many countries can you hear?( )

A. Five. B. Four.

(2) What are they?( )

They are ________.( )

A. China B. Australia C. America

D. Canada E. France F. Japan

4. T: Let's listen again and circle.

(1) Andy is from (America / Canada). He likes (taking pictures / playing football).

(2) Alice likes (making models / making cards).

(3) You can make a model of (Eiffel Tower / Big Ben) in France.

(4) Harry likes drawing pictures. He's from (Canada / America).

(5) Joy is an Australian (girl / boy). You can enjoy lots of (music / art) shows in her country.

5. T: Let's listen to the whole passage again and fill in the blanks.

Name	Countries	Hobbies	Activities
Andy			
Alice			
Harry			
Joy			

6. T: Listen to the whole passage again and talk about the table.

7. T: What's the passage about?

课程设计者：珠海市三灶镇中心小学　何瑞妮

本文以 Jenny 介绍自己不同国家的朋友为主线，谈论不同国家的标志性建筑及有趣的事情，帮助学生了解不同国家的情况。

创编对话整合了几个不同主题的知识点，包括国家、爱好、标志性建筑和活动。本册书在前几个小主题的基础上，从以社区为单位细化到社区中个体的兴趣爱好及时间的安排，最后扩展到不同国家的人有不同的兴趣爱好及时间安排等。以国家为主线，介绍它们的标志性建筑及人们常做的活动。在听说训练前，引导学生猜测 Jenny 朋友的爱好、国籍和不同的国家有什么标志性建筑，让学生思考在这些国家可以做什么有趣的事情，激活学生的旧知和已有的生活经验，为接下来的听说活动做准备。

在听说过程中，先听取关键信息，再引导学生进行一系列的思考，帮助学生谈论不同国家的标志性建筑及有趣的事情，以及不同国家的情况，进一步培养学生的英语综合运用能力。

听说后再引导学生通过问答、填表或描述其中一个国家，并让不同层次的学生去练习口头表达。在这一过程中，学生需要在理解的基础上去分析、应用、总结和表达，培养看图获取信息能力及文本整体输出意识，达到深度学习的目的。

五年级主题 1　Classmates

听力材料

At the school gate. I'm standing in line and waiting for the bus with my classmates. My name is Linda. I'm tall and I have red hair. Can you see me? We are so happy today because we are going to the zoo. There are so many cute animals, such as tigers, hippos, zebras, giraffes and lions ...They are popular, too.

On the bus. Tina is polite and friendly. She asks Eric to get on the bus first. Next, she brings him a paper bag because Eric doesn't feel well on the bus. What about the others? Look, some boys are listening to the music. Some girls are sleeping. All of them are quiet.

In the zoo. Peter is active. He's jumping up and down like a monkey. Bill is telling us about the habits of bears and wolves. He likes reading books about animals. He's clever. Tom is putting a toy snake on Joe's shoulder. How naughty he is! John is picking up all the rubbish we left. And he often helps parents do housework at home. What a helpful boy!

It's time to go back to school. Andy is crying. What happened? He can't find his glasses. Careless Andy! He often loses something.

听说活动

1.Listen and choose.

听力材料：

At the school gate. I'm standing in line and waiting for the bus with my classmates. My name is Linda. I'm tall and I have red hair. Can you see me? We are so happy today because we are going to the zoo. There are so many cute animals, such as tigers, hippos, zebras, giraffes and lions ...They are popular, too.

(1) T: Listen and guess who is Linda?（　　）

A.　　B.　　C.　　D.

(2) What are the animals like in the zoo?（　　）

A. cute　　B. crazy　　C. popular　　D. polite

2. Listen and judge "T"or "F".

听力材料：

On the bus. Tina is polite and friendly. She asks Eric to get on the bus first. Next, she brings him a paper bag because Eric doesn't feel well on the bus. What about the others? Look, some boys are listening to the music. Some girls are sleeping. All of them are quiet.

(1) Tina is polite and friendly because she helps Eric. __________

(2) Eric feels well on the bus. __________

(3) The boys are singing and the girls are dancing. All of them are quiet. __________

3. Listen and tick.

听力材料：

In the zoo. Peter is active. He's jumping up and down like a monkey. Bill is telling us about the habits of bears and wolves. He likes reading books about animals. He's clever. Tom is putting a toy snake on Joe's shoulder. How naughty he is! John is picking up all the rubbish we left. And he often helps parents do housework at home. What a helpful boy! It's time to go back to school. Andy is crying. What happened? He can't find his glasses. Careless Andy! He often loses something.

	clever	careless	quiet	friendly	naughty	active	polite	cute	helpful
Peter						√			
Bill									
Tom									
John									
Andy									

4. Let's say.

(1) Choose one of Linda's classmates and talk about her or him.

Tina

Peter

Bill

Tom

John

Andy

(2) Please talk about Linda's classmates:

Whom do you like best? Why?

Whose behavior is not good? What do you think of it?

What are your classmates like? Can you introduce them?

课程设计者：珠海市香洲区甄贤小学 魏莉

听力文本的主题 Classmates 是学生非常熟悉的话题，它把人物和形容词重新整合为一个完整的故事，贴近日常生活，为学生提供了深度学习的平台，激发学生浓厚的学习兴趣。

听说训练过程中，学生不仅要听懂全文，还要听取细节；运用思维推理能力，明确每个同学的特点；学生对文本的语言输出，促进了语言能力发展和情感体验，实现语言知识和语言技能的迁移和运用。

听说活动 1：第一个问题让学生通过听外貌的描述确定人物，第二个问题让学生边听边联想和回忆动物园里的动物形象，总结归纳动物的特点。

听说活动 2：学生通过听文本，分析和判断人物的特点及状态，锻炼了推理能力。

听说活动 3：学生需要耐心听懂每个人物的行为，细心梳理每个人物的特点，并进行匹配。

口语活动 4：第一题的图片激活了学生大脑中 Linda 同学的影像。学生根据图片的提示，用自己的话描述 Linda 同学的具体行为和特点。第二题是对 Linda 同学的点评，激发学生的情感体验，培养学生的批判性思维，帮他们树立正确的价值观。第三题学生通过思考、总结和描述自己的同学，提升了语言综合运用能力，达成了深度学习的目的。

五年级主题 2 Teachers

听力材料

Voting for My Favorite Teacher

Butts Road Primary School invites all the students to vote for their favorite teacher every year. Some students are talking about their favourite teacher. Now let's listen.

Johnson: My favourite teacher is Mr. Black. He teaches us history. He is short but strong. He wears glasses. He is old and bald, but we never laugh at his bald head. He plays the guitar very well. We have lots of fun in his class.

Lisa: I like Ms. White best. She teaches math. She wears glasses and she looks very strict. But her class is very interesting, so we are not afraid of her. We learn a lot from her math class.

George: I will vote for Mr. Smith. He is my English teacher. He is tall and handsome. He has short orange hair. And he likes wearing suit. He's a very kind teacher. He never shouts at us. I like him.

May: My favourite teacher is Miss Wilson. She is a super star in my heart. She has long blonde curly hair. And she is tall and slim. Do you know how she keeps fit? Right, she dances. I like her dancing class very much. She is nice to all of us.

Kevin: Mr. Tucker is my art teacher. I will vote for him. He is a handsome young man. He always wears shirt and jeans. And he has a pair of red glasses. It looks a little bit funny. Mr. Tucker is a friendly teacher. I like him.

Sarah: Mrs. Fish is from China. She is my Chinese teacher. She is old but graceful. She has short white hair and wears a pair of round glasses. I like to listen to the interesting stories in her class.

听说活动

1. Listen and choose.

A. Mr. Black　　B. Ms. White　　C. Mr. Smith

D. Miss Wilson　　E. Mr. Tucker　　F. Mrs. Fish

(　　)

(　　)

(　　)

(　　)

(　　)

(　　)

2. Listen and tick the four right descriptions.

Mr. Black	Ms. White	Mr. Smith
□ tall	□ tall	□ tall
□ short	□ wear glasses	□ handsome
□ thin	□ slim	□ short orange hair
□ wears glasses	□ strict	□ wears glasses
□ teaches history	□ teaches math	□ teaches Chinese
□ young	□ interesting	□ old
□ bald	□ young	□ kind
Miss Wilson	**Mr. Tucker**	**Mrs. Fish**
□ long curly hair	□ tall	□ tall
□ tall	□ handsome	□ graceful
□ strong	□ young	□ young
□ slim	□ wears jeans	□ wears glasses
□ sing	□ teaches PE.	□ teaches Chinese
□ strict	□ boring	□ old
□ nice	□ friendly	□ pretty

3. Which teacher will win in this year's "My Favourite Teacher" activity? Please talk in your small group.

课程设计者：珠海市横琴新区第一小学　陈丽娜

本单元是贴近学生生活的教师主题。听力材料以“我最喜爱的教师”投票活动拉开帷幕，通过聆听不同学生描述自己最喜欢的教师，完成两个听说活动——人名图片配对题和勾选描述题。第一个活动帮助学生理解文意，根据描述选择正确图片；第二个活动帮助学生聚焦关键词，拓展新词，为后面的口语活动做好词汇句型知识材料铺垫。

通过单元整体学习和两遍听力文本的输入，学生接下来要完成口语实践活动。根据六位同学的描述，你认为哪位教师最有优势，可以高票获选“我最喜爱的教师”呢？学生要观察各位老师的特点和优势，用已学语言说出自己的观点。

五年级主题 3 Animals

听力材料

The animals in Happy Forest are so excited recently. Why? Because they are going to have a sports meet at weekends. The elephant, the horse, the panda, the monkey, the sheep, the bee, the butterfly and the pig. Everyone wants to join the sports meet and get a good result.

Look! Mr. Elephant is so strong! He is going to join the swimming competition because his favourite sport is swimming. This is Mr. Horse. He is going to join the running competition. He can run fast.

Here comes a black and white animal. Do you know who she is? Great! She is Miss Panda. She is going to join the climbing competition with Miss Monkey. She wants to win the competition.

Listen! *"Baa baa black sheep, have you any wool? Yes, sir! Yes, sir! Three bags full"* Who is singing? It's Miss Sheep. She is going to join the singing competition with Miss Bee and Miss Butterfly. They are all good at singing.

What about Mr. Pig? Oh, he is eating a lot of hamburgers. He is going to join the eating competition.

听说活动

1. T: Listen to the first paragraph and guess what the topic is about.

A. Forest animals

B. Animals sports meet

C. Animals in the zoo

2. T: How do you know it is about them? What key words did you hear?

3. T: Let's listen to the whole passage and match the pictures.

(1) 

(2) 

(3) 

(4) 

(5) 

- running competition
- swimming competition
- eating competition
- climbing competition
- singing competition

4. T: Let's listen to the whole passage again and put the right pictures in the blanks.

A　B　C　D　E

5. T: Listen to the whole passage again and pick out the animals and sport words you hear.

教师给每个分好的小组发一个信封，装入一些动物名字的单词和相应的运动项目，其中包含语篇中的下划线单词。学生将再一次听完整个语篇，在听的过程中，小组内进行 Pick up the Words 的竞赛，把听到的动物名字和运动名称挑出来并匹配，看谁挑得多。这些名字就是听力文本的关键词，教师邀请学生把关键词贴在相应的图画上，学生根据图画的情节和关键词所搭建的脚手架，用自己的话简单地说出每个细节，最终串联起整个故事。

6. T: Listen, read and answer.

课程设计者：珠海市香洲区容闳学校 区秋昌

本课主题为 Animals，通过创设森林动物们报名运动会的情景，把本单元的词汇和语法点巧妙地加入听力文本，再配上可爱的连环画，在英语课堂中，勾起学生对学习的好奇心。故事编排合理，情节有趣，内容比较全面，引发学生浓厚的学习兴趣。

创编文本融合了本单元的知识点，包括一般将来时、形容词的使用、个人喜好和情感态度的表达。以它为蓝本开展听说学习，突出学科语言和学科思维。听说训练过程中，听取细节线索，唤醒学生思维能力和推理能力，同时也注重完整不间断的听力输入，触发学生进行连续性的思考，有利于培养学生的逻辑思维，有效提高学生的语言知识学习和听说能力。

把听力输入的语言，用作口头看图说话或复述故事情节，在这过程中，学生需要一次次深刻地进行思考、总结和表达，从而有效整合语言知识和语言技能，提升思维能力和概括能力，达到深度学习的目的。

五年级主题 4　Shopping Day

听力材料

There is a charity sale on Monday in Happy School. All the teachers and students are happy and excited. Let's see what they want to buy.

Bill wants to buy some stationaries. He wants to buy a pen, a pencil box and a box of crayons. The pen is 3 yuan. The pencil box is 10 yuan and the box of crayons is 9 yuan.

Joy wants to buy some stationaries too. She wants to buy a pink ruler, a pink pen and a pink schoolbag. She likes pink very much. The ruler is 2 yuan, the pen is 3 yuan and the school bag is 60 yuan.

Andy wants to buy a toy car for his friend Binbin, because tomorrow is Binbin's birthday. There are two model cars on the charity sale. One is red, the other is blue. The red model car is 50 yuan. The blue one is 90 yuan. He takes the red model car because Binbin's favourite colour is red.

What does Miss Wu want to buy? She wants to buy some story books for her students. She buys 10 storybooks. They are 100 yuan.

They all have a good time on the charity sale.

听说活动

1. T: Listen to the first paragraph and guess what the topic is about.

A. School Charity Sale

B. School Open Day

C. School Sports Day

2. T: How do you know it is about them? What key words did you hear?

3. T: Let's listen to the whole passage and match the pictures.

(1) 

■ 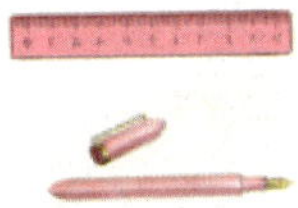 

(2) 

■ 

(3) 

■ 

(4) 

_______________________________. 

4. T: Let's listen to the whole passage again and write down the prices for each goods.

(1)  ¥ ________  ¥ ________  ¥ ________

(2)  ¥ ________  ¥ ________  ¥ ________

(3)  ¥ ________  ¥ ________

(4)  ¥ ________

5. T: Listen to the whole passage again and judge "T" or "F".

(1) There is a charity sale on Friday in Happy School. (   )

(2) Bill buys a pencil, a pencil box and a box of crayons. (   )

(3) The pink schoolbag is 16 yuan. (   )

(4) Binbin likes red. (   )

(5) Miss Wu wants to buy some story books. (   )

6. T: Listen, read and answer.

(1) Are the teachers and students happy and excited on Monday?

____

(2) What does Bill buy on the Charity Sale?

____

(3) How much does Joy pay for the stationaries?

____

(4) Why does Andy choose the red car?

____

(5) How many books does Miss Wu buy?

____

课程设计者：珠海市香洲区容闳学校 区秋昌

本课程以学校举办的慈善义卖为主线，通过介绍学生熟悉的人物购买的物品、数量和价格的听力文本整合改编，再配上学生熟悉的人物插图，在英语课堂中，激起学生对本单元知识点的回顾。文本编排合理有趣，富有科学道理，引发学生浓厚的学习兴趣。

创编文本融合了几个不同主题的知识点，包括名词单复数、量词、颜色、第三人称单数的动词变化和情感态度的表达。文本以学校奉办慈善义卖师生的购物情景为蓝本，开展听说学习，突出学科语言和学科思维。听说训练过程中，听取细节线索，唤醒思维和推理能力，同时也注重完整不间断的听力输入，有利于培养学生的逻辑思维，提高学生的语言知识学习和听说能力。

把听力输入的语言，用作口头看图说话或复述义卖购物情节，在这个过程中，学生需要一次次深刻地进行思考、总结和表达，从而有效整合了语言知识和语言技能，提升了思维概括能力，达到深度学习的目的。

五年级主题 5 TV Shows

听力材料

My name is Xiaomei. My favorite TV show is the **variety show-Running Man**. This is an outdoor competitive show hosted by seven stars. They go to different places to complete different tasks. I like running and playing games. I like watching this show very much. I usually watch it on Fridays.

My father's hobby is very different from mine. He likes watching **sports shows**. He likes watching CCTVs' sports channel 5 best. In CCTV5, he can enjoy the news and competitions of all kinds of sports. He likes all kinds of sports. He usually watches it on Saturdays and Sundays.

My mother likes **music show-Sing**! **China**. My mother can sing. She likes music and singing. Through this show, she can enjoy more wonderful music. She usually watches this on Sundays.

We have different interests, but we are modest to each other. My mother and I usually accompany my father to watch **sports shows**. My father and I usually accompany my mother to watch **music shows**. And my parents usually accompany me to watch **variety shows**. We love each other.

听说活动

1. T: Listen to the passage and say what the topic is about.

2. T: How many characters are there in the passage? Who are they?

3. T: Let's listen to the whole passage and match.

CCTV 5
体育

4. T: Let's listen to the whole passage again and summarize.

Who?	What?	Why?
Xiaomei	Running man	He likes running and playing games.
Xiaomei's father		
Xiaomei's mother		

5. T: Listen to the whole passage again and fill in the blanks.

- Xiaomei usually watches Running man on ____________ .

- Xiaomei's father usually watches CCTV5 on ________ and ________.
- Xiaomei's mother usually watches Sing!China on __________ .

6. T: Listen and read the passage and answer the questions.

(1) What's your favorite TV show?

(2) When do you usually watch it?

(3) Why do you like it?

课程设计者：珠海市香洲区甄贤小学　彭钦

孩子们最熟悉的人除了自己就是父母了，本听力文本中的小梅描述了自己与父母对于电视节目的不同兴趣，与我们分享了大家熟悉的三种电视节目：综艺《奔跑吧》、体育频道 CCTV5 和音乐节目《中国好声音》。文本从学生身边的事情出发、从学生喜闻乐见的情境出发，再现生活实际，引起学生的兴趣。

创编文本融合了几个不同的知识点，包括 like 后的动词加 ing 以及一般现在时。以它为蓝本开展听说学习，突出学科语言和学科思维。听说训练中，先听材料，把人物和他们喜欢的电视节目匹配；再听重点，完成表格，并总结人物喜欢这类电视节目的原因；然后听细节，完成句子。活动的设计体现了层次性和递进性，活动与活动之间紧密相连，能锻炼学生的信息提取能力。

最后根据学生的实际情况，提出了三个问题，引发学生思考，鼓励学生用英语表达所想。学生在课堂中运用英语进行表达的过程就是用英语思考的过程，有利于其进行深度学习，提高他们的学习能力。

五年级主题 6　Chores

听力材料

May 1st, Saturday

I'm Xiaohua. Xiaoming is my good friend. We're neighbors, so we usually talk on the way home. Today we talked about what we would do when we were at home.

Xiaoming said that he would make the bed every morning and usually take out the trash at night. He takes out the trash three times a week. He cleans the desk after finishing the homework every day. He usually cleans the room, sweeps the floor and washes the clothes on weekends. He cleans the room once a week. He sweeps the floor twice a week and he washes the clothes once a week.

But I usually watch TV in the living room at night every day, or play chess with my father. After dinner, I usually do my homework in my bedroom. On weekends, I usually go to the park and play with my friends. I didn't do any chores at home.

I learn a lot from Xiaoming. I change a lot at home now. What can you learn from Xiaoming?

听说活动

1. T: Listen to the passage and say what the topic is about.

2. T: How do you know it is about them? What key words did you hear?

3. T: Let's listen to the whole passage and choose the relationships of Xiaohua and Xiaoming.

(　) (　) (　)

4. T: Let's listen to the whole passage again and summarize what chores Xiaoming does at home.

What?	How often?
make the bed	every morning

5. T: Listen to the whole passage again and talk:

What changes does Xiaohua have? What can you learn from Xiaoming?

教师提前给学生分组（一般 3 ~ 4 人一组），小组讨论小华到底有了哪些改变。本题为开放性题目，同学们可以各抒己见，这样有利于锻炼学生的思维能力和表达能力。

6. T: Listen and read the passage and answer the questions.

- Do you usually do chores at home? What chores do you usually do at home?
- How often do you do chores?
- Do you really like doing chores? Why do you do chores at home?

课程设计者：珠海市香洲区甄贤小学 彭钦

本听力文本通过聆听一位小学生的生活日记，引发学生对于家庭劳动的一系列思考。Xiaohua 的日记描述了自己最好的朋友 Xiaoming 在家经常帮家人做家务，而自己每天贪玩，也比较懒散。该情景创设非常生活化，能有效激发学生的学习兴趣，使其积极主动地参与课堂教学活动，还能够引起他们的共鸣，让他们对自己的日常生活产生思考，有一定的教育意义。

创编文本融合了几个不同的知识点，包括一般现在时和频率词的使用。以它为蓝本开展听说学习，突出学科语言和学科思维。听说训练过程中，先听材料提取文章大意，再听细节，引导学生完成表格，注重提升学生的信息提取能力和概括能力。

创设活动让学生积极参与讨论，与同学分享自己的想法，培养学生的逻辑思维、创新思维及批判思维。最后，让学生运用所学知识进行英语表达，锻炼学生的思维能力和表达能力，进而整合语言知识和语言技能，达到深度学习的目的。

五年级主题 7 Keeping Healthy

听力材料

Tim has a health check in the hospital. After the checkup, the doctor talks with him.

Doctor: Tim, you are not healthy. You are overweight. How do you feel these days?

Tim: Well, I feel tired. I always sleep in class. I'm not hungry, but I want to eat more.

Doctor: What food do you like eating?

Tim: I like eating meat and hamburgers every day. They are yummy.

Doctor: Do you often eat vegetables or fruit?

Tim: No, I don't like them.

Doctor: What do you like doing at home?

Tim: I often watching TV for a long time at home.

Doctor: So you often stay up late. Right?

Tim: Yes. I often go to bed at midnight.

Doctor: Well, I know why you often sleep in class. That's too bad for you.

Tim: I want to be healthy. What should I do?

Doctor: First, you should eat **healthy food**. You **should eat a lot of**

vegetables and fruit every day. You **shouldn't eat too much meat**.

Tim: Can I eat hamburgers? I love hamburgers.

Doctor: Oh, sometimes you can eat a little, but not very often. And you **should go to bed at 9:30p.m. Don't watch too much TV**.

Tim: OK.

Doctor: And you **should exercise every day**.

Tim: But I don't like sports.

Doctor: Come on. Maybe you can **play basketball** or **run** with your friends. Then you'll feel good! And you'll be handsome and healthy soon.

Tim: OK. I'll try to do my best!

Then the doctor makes the healthy check report for Tim.

听说活动

1. Where is Tim? (　　)

A. 

B. 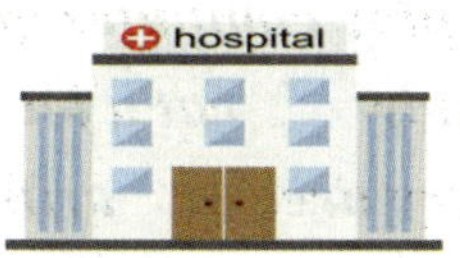

C. 

2. What's the matter with Tim? Can you tell?

3. Listen to the whole dialogue and number the pictures.

( ) ( ) ( ) ( )

( ) ( ) ( ) ( )

4. Listen to the dialogue again, circle the phrases you hear and talk about the pictures with these phrases.

watch too much TV *brush your teeth* *eat some meat*
get up early *play computer games* *run*
eat too much candy *eat a lot of fruit* *stay in bed*
play soccer *every tired* *drink a lot of water*
exercise every day *see the dentist* *drink some milk*
eat too much hamburgers *wash your hands*
take some medicine *go to bed at 9:30* *swim*
sleep in class *drink some juice* *eat too much meat*
eat a lot of vegetables *play basketball* *stay up late*

5. Speaking: What should we do to keep healthy?

(Before speaking, please read the phrases you have circled first.)

–We should...

–We shouldn't...

课程设计者：珠海市平沙镇中心小学　李锦嫦

由于人们的生活水平普遍提高，很多大在享受生活时，忽略了一些日常坏习惯，而它们正危害着我们的健康。健康是我们关注的问题，定期做体检已成常态。在这样的背景下，学习真实的语言，进行自然的健康教育符合英语课标中的语言学习目标。

此文本以 Tim 到医院做定期体检作为本单元“Keeping Healthy”这一话题的引线，通过 Doctor 和 Tim 的对话，找出 Tim 身体不健康的原因并给出有效建议。以它为蓝本开展听说学习，突出学科语言和学科思维。本听说材料是对五年级主题 7 Keeping Healthy 内容的拓展。主要通过有梯度的听说活动，慢慢引导学生由专注听材料内容过渡到关于生活习惯问题的思考和正确运用语言表达等方面。这些做法对英语思维的逻辑性、批判性和发散性有一定的提升。

具体表现为：

听说活动 1：猜地点，引导学生了解要谈论的话题，激发兴趣，为接下来的活动做好准备。

听说活动 2：通过语音输入，大概了解谈论的话题和内容。

听说活动 3：再听文本，更注重细节上的听和思考，让学生读懂和学习文本内容。

听说活动 4：再听文本，注重短语的习得和运用，选短语说句子，复述文本故事，使语言得以输出。

听说活动 5：朗读听说活动 4 列出的短语，对生活中保持健康的话题做进一步的了解和讨论，生成自己要输出的语言。

五年级主题 8 Special Day

听力材料

1. **New Year's Day** is on January 1st. We can have a big dinner with our family on that day. **Tree Planting Day** is on March 12th, and we can plant trees in the garden! I like it so much. On June 1st, it's **Children's Day**! It's our day. We can have a big party with our friends and enjoy a cake. What about **Teachers' Day**? It's on September 10th. On that day, we will make greeting cards and send them to teachers. What's my favourite day? Let me tell you. It's **Christmas Day**! It's on December 25th. We can get many presents and have a big Christmas party. That's interesting!

2. This festival is in January or February. People can get together and enjoy the day. Before that day, my parents will clean our house. My mother will make dumplings with me! I like eating dumplings. In the evening, family will have a big dinner together. Children can set off fireworks. They will be so happy. During this festival, children can wear the new clothes. It means good luck. Also, children can get red packets from the family. What a happy festival!

听说活动

1. Listen and circle the special day.

听文本 1，圈出文中提及的各节日的信息。此项练习，能够锻炼学生提取关键信息的能力。

Children's Day　Christmas Day　Mother's Day　Tree Planting Day

National Day　Dragon Boat Festival　New Year's Day　Teachers' Day

2. Listen and write down the activity of special day.

再听文本 1，学生在听的过程中归纳各个节日所涉及的不同活动，提升学生信息归纳和总结信息的能力。

(1) Tree Planting Day　______________________

(2) Children's Day　______________________

(3) Teachers' Day　______________________

(4) Christmas Day　______________________

3. Listen and guess the festival.

听文本 2，提取关键信息，推测相关节日。

Question: What festival is it? ______________________.

4. Listen and number the picture.

通过再听文本 2，抓住重点信息并给下列图片编号，引导学生记关键词，以小组为单位用自己的语言讲述节日活动。

(　)

(　)

(　)

(　)

(　)

(　)

5. Talk in pairs about your favorite day.

通过之前的听力文本学习，学生对 special day 和各活动已有一定的认识。教师在此部分设置相应的口语对话练习，让学生根据 message box 的提示进行对话练习，谈论自己喜欢的节日和活动。

Mid -Autumn Festival	make a snowman
Christmas	play games
Spring Festival	watch the moon
Children's Day	get some red packets
National Day	have a big dinner
	get some presents
	have a party
	have fun

Tony: Hello, Jenny. What's your favorite day?

Jenny: My favorite day is ______________. I can ________. What about you?

Tony: That's interesting! I like ____________. I can ____________.

Tony& Jenny: Great! Let's play together.

课程设计者：珠海市平沙镇中心小学　周沁妍

《义务教育英语课程标准（2022年版）》指出，英语课程要培养的学生核心素养包括语言能力、文化意识、思维品质和学习能力等方面。核心素养的四个方面相互渗透，融合互动，协同发展。

基于此，本节听说课围绕Special Day这一主题展开教学，由几个关于节日的不同文本串联而成，以语篇文本为依托，通过学习理解、应用实践和迁移创新等活动铺陈出中国传统节日及传统的习俗，引导学生在听说文本的学习中整合性地学习语言知识和中国传统节日的文化知识。通过此听说课程的输入，学生将在听说文本中学会提取、思考、归纳信息，提炼语篇中的结构化知识，进而运用所学知识、技能和策略，围绕传统节日的主题表达个人观点和想法，解决实际问题，达到在教学中培养学生核心素养的目的。同时，在此基础上，以多层次、多角度来分析本节课中的语篇所传递的意义，挖掘中国传统文化内涵和育人价值，把握教学主线，渗透育人教学，提高学生的民族自豪感。

五年级主题9 Making Contact

听力材料

Hurrah! The Lantern Festival is coming. David, Lisa and Andy are making **a phone call**. They want to do some interesting things.

Hello, I'm Mike. I am in Harbin. On the Lantern Festival, I can go to Harbin Ice and Snow World with my parents after eating Yuanxiao. We can see some colorful lights there. They are wonderful! My mother wants to take some photos. My father wants to **send an email** to our relatives in Singapore. It is a different world. So amazing!

Hi, My name is Amy. I am in Chaozhou. On the Lantern Festival, I can eat tangyuan with my family. After that, I want to **make a video call** to my classmates in Guangzhuo. We can watch the dragon lantern dance and enjoy the fireworks.

Hello, I'm John. I'm in Shanghai. On the Lantern Festival, Children here can play in the street with self-made or bought lanterns. They are excited. On that time, I want to **send a short message** to my friends. We can guess the lantern riddles together. It's very interesting. My brother wants to **write letters**. They are about the riddles. Then he post the letters on the lanterns. You can check the answer to him. If you are right, he will mail a present to you.

听说活动

1. T: Listen and guess what the topic is about. (　　)

A. The Lantern Festival

B. Ice and Snow Festival

C. Dragon Boat Festival

2. T: Listen again and find out which Child is in Shanghai. (　　)

A. John　　　　B. Mike　　　　C. Amy

3. T: Listen to the second paragraph, then answer the questions.

(1) On Lantern Festival, where does Mike want to go?

(2) What does Mike's father want to do?

4. T: Listen to the third paragraph, then answer the questions.

(1) Amy is in Chaozhou. Can Amy see the Ice Light there ?

(2) How do the people celebrate the Lantern Festival in Chaozhou?

(3) Amy's classmates are in Guangzhou. Can they watch the dragon lantern dance on Lantern Festival? How can they see it?

5. T: Listen to the last paragraph, then talk about how to celebrate the Lantern Festival in Shanghai.

6. T: How many ways of the contact are there in this passage ? What are they?

课程设计者：珠海市香洲区第十一小学 韩红霞

在英语教学中进行中国传统文化的渗透，不仅是英语跨文化交际能力培养的一项重要任务，也是将中国传统文化对外传播的一种重要手段。在英语课堂教学中，缺少了中国文化的渗透，会影响学习者在语言实践中对中国文化的诠释和表达。所以，在英语教学的过程中，应该对中国传统文化进行有效的渗透，这样不仅有助于更好地培养学习者的跨文化交际能力，还有助于中国传统文化的保留、延续与传播。

本单元的主题是“Making Contact”。本次听说课的设计是将生活中的各种联系方式和中国传统节日——元宵节的各项风俗融合在一起。渗透同一个节日在不同地域风俗习惯的不同：即便是同一种食物，北方称元宵，南方称汤圆。由于通讯的发达，我们可以根据实际需要选择不同的方式与家人和朋友保持联系，分享幸福、快乐时光。

五年级主题 10 Have a Great Trip

听力材料

On October 3rd, we went to Jinwan Zhuhai by car. We watched the 13th Airshow China there. It was the last day of the Airshow. The weather was sunny and hot. The sky was blue.

The planes climbed, flipped, and danced above our head. It was so great! We saw "August 1st " Team at 11:20 a.m. Aerospace CAIHONG CH−4 flew at 11:50 a.m. Our Zhuhai Airlines came out at last at 1:10 p.m. The shows were wonderful.

And then, in the afternoon, we saw many guns, tanks, and spaceship models in the exhibition, too.

Then we had a big afternoon tea at McDonald's in the airport. The hamburgers and chicken were spicy but tasty. In the restaurant, we met a captain. We talked a lot. He liked Zhuhai's Airshow very much.

听说活动

1. Look at the picture, guess and answer the following questions.

2. Listen and choose the car Dad drove to the Airshow. (　　)

A. 粤 C WJ 522　　B. 粤 C JV 123　　C. 粤 C 8888B

3. Listen and write down the time of each show.

　:

　:

　:

4. Listen to the whole passage and order the pictures.

(　　)

(　　)

(　　)

(　　)

(　　)

(　　)

5. Pair work: Suppose you and your partner were Gogo and captain, please discuss and fulfill the dialogue.

6.

Make your own talk with your partner.

Gogo: Where are you from?
Captain: I'm from ________.
Gogo: Where were you last week?
Captain: I was in ________.
Gogo: What was the _______ like in _______?
Captain: It was ____________.
Gogo: Do you like the Airshow?
Captain: Yes. The show is _______. Zhuhai is ________. China is ________.

课程设计者：珠海市香洲区第一小学　简臻红

在珠海举办的中国国际航空航天博览会（中国航展）是珠海闪亮的一张名片，它见证了我国国防现代化事业突飞猛进，国防力量厚积薄发。学习围绕此主题创编的听说文本，使学生在学习英语的同时，增强民族自信心，对本土文化产生强烈的认同感和自豪感。

课程开始教师通过让学生观察图片信息和回答简单的问题，初步了解主题情境。为了引起学生对故事的好奇，带着未能解决的问题“What was the date？”进入文本。众所周知，2021年航展期间，珠海大道按日期的单双号限制车辆通行，通过提取所听到的主人公出发去航展的日期信息，选出适合他们出行的车辆，唤醒学生的推理能力，让他们通过英语学习，解决现实生活中的实际问题。

听取并记录各飞行表演的具体时间，锻炼学生听取细节信息的能力。听全文，根据短文内容的先后顺序给图片排序，锻炼了学生通过专注聆听，整体了解文本结构和概况的能力。通过不同方式的听力训练，学生掌握了听力技巧与策略，并感受文本中蕴含的“中国制造”的力量。

课程最后，假设学生和同桌是Gogo和机长，学生在教师的引导下，按照对话框架自编语言，聊聊天。学生在合作中提升了口语表达能力，锻炼了发散性思维和逻辑思维。在主题情境的引领下，最后学生自然而然发出“The show is <u>nice</u>. Zhuhai is <u>great</u>. China is <u>strong</u>.”的感叹，体现了他们的爱国主义情怀。

五年级主题 11 Have a Magical Trip

听力材料

My trip <u>was</u> magic. I <u>flew</u> back home for a long time in the sky with Big Black. We <u>were</u> tired, hungry and thirsty. We couldn't find any water.

Big Black <u>said</u> he <u>could</u> do me a magic. Then, he <u>told</u> me to stop in a waxberry tree. He <u>asked</u> me to look around. I <u>saw</u> many green fruits on it. Soon, I was not thirsty at all. How amazing it was! At last, we <u>ate</u> some. They were yucky and sour.

We flew over mountains. We were really thirsty and sad. Suddenly, we <u>found</u> a bottle of water and I was excited, but there wasn't much water in it. I couldn't drink it. Big Black <u>did</u> a magic again. Can you guess what the magic was?

Big Black <u>brought</u> back some stones and he <u>put</u> them into the bottle. The water <u>rose</u>. How magical it was! We <u>drank</u> some and then put more stones in it. Finally, we drank all of it.

So, happily we <u>got</u> home. My mother was very happy to see me. She <u>gave</u> me a lot of good food and asked me a lot of questions.

听说活动

1. T: Listen to the first paragraph and guess what the story is about.

A. Rabbits B. Cocks C. Crows

2. T: How do you know it is about them? What key words did you hear?

教师播放第一段听力内容：My trip was magic. I flew back home for a long time in the sky with Big Black. We were tired, hungry and thirsty. We couldns't find any water. 播放后，学生根据听到的关键词 flew, in the sky, black 做出判断选择：名字叫 Big Black 的动物颜色很有可能是外表为黑色的动物，由此可以排除 A 项“白兔”；虽然 B 项和 C 项都是黑色的动物，但是根据关键词 flew 和 in the sky 得知主角是能在天上飞的动物，比较公鸡和乌鸦，不难判断乌鸦比公鸡更善于在天空飞翔，因此可排除 B 项。由此可见，引导学生听取细节线索，能唤醒学生的推理能力，提升他们思维的灵敏性。

3. T: Let's listen to the whole passage and number the pictures.

(　　)

(　　)

(　　)

(　　)

4. T: Let's listen to the whole passage again and put the right pictures in the blanks.

1 2 3 4 5 6

5. T: Listen to the whole passage again and pick out the past tense words you hear.

教师给每个分好的小组发一个信封，装入一些不规则动词的过去式的动词，其中包含语篇中下划线的单词。学生将再一次听整个语篇，在听的过程中，小组内进行 Pick up the Words 的竞赛，把听到文本中的不规则动词的过去式挑出来，看谁挑得多。这些动词就是听力文本的关键词，教师邀请学生把关键词贴在相应的图画上，学生根据图画的情节和关键词所搭建的脚手架，用自己的话简单说出每个细节，最终串联起整个故事。

6. T: Listen, read the story and answer Mom's questions.

(1) How was your trip?

(2) What happened next?

(3) Were you happy, then? Why?

(4)What was the magic?

教师展示乌鸦兄弟到家与妈妈聊天的图片，关于旅途中发生的趣事，教师扮演乌鸦妈妈问了以上几个问题，在听力后继续深挖学生的听力输入，学生代入乌鸦兄弟的角色思考、回答乌鸦妈妈对他们的提问。学生在完成前面一系列听说任务的基础上，在一定的情境中，再次自然地整体重构文本内容，深化故事的文本内涵，体验故事带来的乐趣。把听力输入的语言，用作口头复述故事情节，在这过程中，学生需要再一次深刻地进行思考、总结和表达。以上两种不同方式的回顾，有效整合了语言知识和语言技能，提升了学生的思维能力和概括能力，达到深度学习的目的。

课程设计者：珠海市香洲区第一小学　简臻红

五年级主题 12　Growing up

听力材料

This is Yuan Longping's growing-up story. He is a very famous Chinese scientist. He is called "Father of Hybrid Rice (杂交水稻)". He grew rice for us ——the people in China and the world.

Yuan Longping was born on September 7th, 1930. He was born in Beijing. He died on May 22nd, 2021.

Yuan Longping learned to speak and walk when he was a little baby. When he grew up, he started to study English with his mother. He went to school in many different cities in China.

When Yuan Longping was a student in Boxue Middle School, he learned to play the violin. He was good at singing, too. He can swim very fast. But he was not good at math.

Yuan Longping was great. We are proud of him. And we love him forever.

听说活动

1. T: Listen to the passage and tell me the passage is mainly about:(　)

A. Yang Liwei's growing up story. | Yang Liwei

B. Yuan Longping's growing up story. | Yuan Longping

C. Qian Xuesen's growing up story. | Qian Xuesen

2. T: Let's listen to the whole passage and number the pictures.

( )

Yuan Longping
( )

Qian Xuesen
( )

( )

( )

( )

3. T: Listen to the passage and fill in the blanks:

(1) Yuan Longping was ____ on September 7th, 1930.

(2) Yuan Longping ____ to speak and walk when he was a little baby.

(3) When he grew up, he ____ to study English with his mother.

(4) When Yuan Longping was a student in Boxue Middle School, he learned to __________.

(5) He can ____ very fast.

4. T: Listen to the whole passage again and try to retell the story in groups.

每个活动小组分得一套图片，学生根据图片提示，小组合作，先排好顺序，然后小组成员根据图片内容，轮流复述文章。小组合作结束后，以小组为单位进行展示汇报。图片可参考第 2 题中的图片。

5. T: Do you like Yuan Longping? Why?

课程设计者：珠海市香洲区广生小学　李丽丽

本单元听力文本以五年级主题 12 Growing up 为背景，以我国“杂交水稻之父”袁隆平先生生平为依据创编。学生在英语学习的同时，了解了国家英雄和伟大科学家，增强了民族自豪感，培养家国情怀，从而树立正确的人生观和价值观。

听力文本以时间为顺序，简单阐述了袁隆平先生的成长故事，其中包含本单元大量的核心词汇。这些词汇学生都已掌握，在不同人物主题中再次出现，能够激发学生应用已学词汇的积极性。以下设计的题目，循序渐进，先泛听确定文章主题，再精听、操练核心信息和重点词汇。复述材料的设计，意在让学生在信息输入之后，能够提取关键信息，进行表达。通过听说训练，学生把袁隆平的成长故事内化为自己的知识，作为自己的知识储备。

六年级主题 1 In China

听力材料

After the journey to the west, Xuanzang wants to know what his partners' experiences when they return to different places.

"Haha, It's me! I am Monkey King. I missed my friends so much. Let me introduce my friends' life to you, my dear master. Friar Sand is still a hardworking man. He went to **Xi'an** to study. He visited the **Terracotta Army** and learned a lot about history by visiting.

Zhubajie still can't change his greedy habit. There are so much delicious food in **Guangdong**, so he went to Guangzhou. He did nothing but enjoyed food. He ate seafood, had **morning tea** and **tasted soup**. Next time I see him, he'll put on weight again.

As the king of Huaguo Mountain, I came back to **Jiangsu** province. I went to **Suzhou** and visited **famous gardens** there. I love there very much. I ate lots of peaches.

My dear master, we miss you a lot. We'll go to **Beijing** to visit you next month. I also want to know more about **Beijing** and your life there."

听说活动

1. Listen and choose.

A.Beijing	B.Lhasa	C.Guangzhou	D.Xi'an	E.Jiangsu

( )   ( )   ( )   ( )

2. Stick and say.

Model: Monkey King is in Jiangsu.

3. Listen and write.

A	B
Xi'an	eat seafood, have morning tea and taste soup
Guangzhou	visit the Terracotta Army
Jiangsu	visit famous gardens

4. Listen, choose and talk.

Model: I am Zhubajie.

I am in Guangzhou.

I can eat much delicious food.

I want to see Canton Tower.

I like swimming and playing in the Water Park.

5.Think and say.

Beijing

- What's it famous for?
- What do you want to do there?

课程设计者：珠海市香洲区第一小学　徐洲丽

本故事以中国四大名著之一《西游记》为背景，以学生喜闻乐见的孙悟空作为故事的讲述者，利用中国地图、图片、音频等多模态教学形式，在英语课堂教学中融合了中国相关传统文化与学生的生活实际，充分发挥英语学科的工具性和人文性，使学生能用英语讲好中国故事，弘扬中国传统文化。

此创编文本主要以孙悟空讲述师徒四人西天取经后在中国的近况作为故事的线索，整合六年级主题 1 的知识要点，让学生在听说训练过程中学会运用过去时态、巩固不规则动词过去式、区分区域地点、介绍名胜古迹和表述情感态度。

听说活动 1：听说活动前老师介绍故事背景和角色，即唐僧师徒四人西天取经回国后发生的故事，以此引发学生的学习兴趣。学生带着任务听第一遍故事，找出孙悟空与师门兄弟三人现在所在的地点，提升学生听力的专注度与对关键地点词汇的掌握度。

口语活动 2：学生在地图上标记故事人物所在地点，并运用英语句型正确表述。此活动既能提升学生的口语表达能力，又能加强他们对中国地理位置的认知。

听说活动 3：学生阅读信息栏，听第二遍故事，把相关信息配对。这训练了学生听取细节信息的能力，加深学生对中国各地文化的了解。

听读活动 4：听第三遍故事，阅读文本，以小组为单位，每位小组成员选择一个故事中的人物，结合人物特征和文本背景，发挥想象，进行表述。根据听说文本，小组分角色表述，培养学生对所学语言知识的表达及小组合作能力。

口语活动 5：假如你是玄奘，说一说你在北京的生活。此活动能拓宽学生的知识面，提升他们语言运用的综合能力。

六年级主题 2　Around the World

听力材料

I'm so excited that I heard a piano song—"Ding dong. Ding dong." My cousin, a four-year-old boy practiced it just now. I knew this song when I was a little child, because I began *to play* the piano at five. This song came from Big Ben in London, England. Later, it developed into an international time-music-The Westminster Quarters (威斯敏斯特钟声). It's just a few simple notes, but it is unusual. The Westminster Quarters were used at Cambridge University (剑桥大学) first, so some people call it the Cambridge Bells.

I really want *to visit* Big Ben in London. My English friend, Tom told me something about it. Big Ben is not the name of a man. It's a name of a clock. It's in London. London is the capital of England. There are four faces of the big clock. So, whenever you stand on the east or west, you can read the face of the clock. The hands of it are about four meters. And I want *to visit* the House of the Parliament. In this place, you will find the Big Ben sitting at the top of the clock tower in the House of the Parliament.

The clock strikes every fifteen minutes- 

.

Every thirty minutes it strikes as- 

.

Every forty–five minutes it strikes as–  .

听说活动

1. T: Listen to the passage and guess what the topic is about.

A. Big Ben　　B. the White House　　C. the Opera House

2. T: How do you know it is about them? What key words did you hear?

3. T: Listen to the first paragraph and judge “T” or “F”.

(1) The little boy who is practicing the piano is five.(　)

(2) The song came from the USA.(　)

(3) The Westminster Quarters (威斯敏斯特钟声) is famous in Cambridge University (剑桥大学).(　)

4. T: Let’s listen to the second paragraph and guess the Chinese meaning of House of the Parliament.

A. 大英博物馆　　B. 白宫　　C. 国会大厦

5. T: Let’s listen to the second paragraph again and match the time and songs. Then try to sing the song in groups.

A	B
every 15 minutes	
every 30 minutes	

every 45 minutes 

在此环节中，教师可让学过钢琴的学生或者熟悉威斯敏斯特钟声作为学校铃声的孩子做向导，带动其他学生兴趣盎然地持续学习。

6. T: Listen to the whole passage again and find out the verbs you hear: underline the past tense and circle the simple present tense. Pay more attention to the third person singular form.

让学生再次听完整语篇，边听边将语篇中出现的动词，尤其是不规则动词的过去式下划线的单词，圈出动词原形，标红动词的第三人称单数形式。这些动词是听力文本的关键词，邀请学生把关键词分类写在黑板上，学生根据板书上的动词和关键词所搭建的脚手架，用自己的语言简单地说出每个段落的故事梗概，最终还原完整语篇。

7. Fill in the blanks according to the passage.

I want to ________the Big Ben in London. There ________four faces. We can _______the face of the clock. The hands of it _______about four meters. The clock _______every fifteen minutes– .

课程设计者：珠海市香洲区第一小学 钟静

我们从小到大，听得最多的上课铃声一定有这个：“灯 — 等 — 灯 — 等——，等 — 灯 — 邓 — 登——”，这段铃声的旋律其实源自英国伦敦的Big Ben，后来发展成一种国际通行的报时音乐——威斯敏斯特钟声。此听力文本从一首简单的练习钢琴曲引出这段钟声。最有意思的地方是，由于每次报时的钟声是不一样的，学生可以根据听到的钟声来判断现在的时间。英语课堂的听说训练，以威斯敏斯特钟声引出对伦敦大本钟的向往，故事编排合理，情节有趣。艺术无国界，经典音乐可以引发学生浓厚的学习兴趣。

此文本融合了以前所学的所有知识点，包括一般现在时、一般过去时的运用、不规则动词过去式的巩固、动词不定式和情感态度的表达。以它为蓝本进行听说训练学习，学生需要一次次深刻地进行思考、总结和表达，从而有效整合了语言知识和语言技能，提升了学生的思维概括能力，使学生达到深度学习的效果，进行多方式“悦”读。在愉悦的氛围中，进行语言的输入，为顺利地“说”奠定基础。在听说训练过程中，听取细节线索，唤醒思维推理能力，同时也注重先整体输入——不间断的听力输入，激发学生进行连续性的思考，有利于培养学生的逻辑思维能力，学生的语言知识学习和听说能力都能得到最有效的提高。在学生语言输出的环节，给学生提供适当的信息，让学生在信息的提示下完成交际活动。1. 功能句型提示。通过板书或多媒体设备为学生提供交流中用到的功能句型，让学生通过信息替换进行英语交流。2. 关键词提示。在交流活动中，列出表达中涉及内容的关键词，让学生依据关键词的提示完成英语交流。3. 图片提示。在讲述事件或复述故事的任务中，呈现一些带有情节的图片，可以帮助学生完整、有条理地进行口语表达，给学生创设宽松的语言交际环境。因此，在输出环节，积极正面鼓励学生勇敢地说，不过分追究他们在语言表达中的瑕疵和欠缺。

六年级主题 3　Animals

听力材料

Can you see **wild animals** like **tigers** or **lions** in Zhuhai? Of course not. What **wild animals** can we see in Zhuhai? Let's find them out !

As a seaside city, we may find many **wild animals** by the sea or on the island. First, there are **Chinese White Dolphins** near Hong Kong–Zhuhai–Macau Bridge. **Dolphins** are mammals. They are white and lovely. They can swim very fast. Mostly, you can see them jumping in and out of the sea.

If you want to see something lovely, you can go to Qi'ao Mangrove. There are lots of **mudskippers** there. Some people call them "**jumping fish**". They are **fish**. They're little, but they have big heads and big eyes. They like jumping on the mud.

Do you know that there is a **monkey** mountain in Zhuhai? It's on Dangan Island. On the mountain, there are many monkeys there. They are brown and yellow. They like climbing trees. Their favorite food is peanut. It's funny!

In Zhuhai, if you take a walk by the sea, you may usually see **little crabs** crawling on the rocks. If you want to see something flying in the sky, you may go to Zhuhai Grand Theater. There are lots of **birds** by the sea. You can sit in a restaurant, have a cup of tea and enjoy the **birds**. Isn't it nice?

听说活动

1. T: Listen to the passage and choose the best topic. (　　)

A. Zhuhai　B. Wild Animals　C. Wild Animals in Zhuhai

2. T: Why did you choose that topic? Can you tell the reasons?

3. T: Let's listen to the passage, number the animals and match the animals to the places you hear.

(　　) 　　

(　　) 　　

(　　) 　　

(　　) 　　

(　　) 　　

4. T: Let's listen to the first and second paragraphs, and circle the words or phrases you hear.

(Repeat steps for the rest paragraphs.)

Paragraph 1 and 2

fish　running
dolphin
Dangan Island　bridge
mammals　crab
white　swim　monkey

Paragraph 3

peanut　Qi'ao
Mangrove　birds
mudskippers　city
little　big　head　eyes
climbing　jumping

Paragraph 4

monkey　Dangan
Island　dolphin
mammals　black
brown　yellow　white
climbing　swimming

Paragraph 5

fish　sea　green　red
dolphin　crabs
flying
Zhuhai　Grand　Theater
birds　jumping

把文本分成四部分（第一、第二段，第三段，第四段，第五段）分别进行活动。学生把听到的单词或短语圈出来，然后在组内进行交流。再次听录音，检查答案。小组分工，每位成员选一种动物，在上面框中词语的帮助下，从外表、特性等方面描述动物。

5. T: Listen to the whole passage again and number the pictures.

( ) ( ) ( ) ( ) ( )

( ) ( ) ( ) ( ) ( )

6. T: Listen and read the story, and then answer the following questions.

- After learning this passage, where do you want to go best to watch the animals?
- What wild animals can you see in Zhuhai? Where can you see them? What do they look like?

课程设计者：珠海市香洲区第一小学 林健仪

本单元主题是动物。学生们对动物都有一定的了解，但珠海并不是一个动物资源丰富的城市，缺乏大型的野生动物。但作为一个美丽的滨海城市，珠海也因沿海地貌特色而有一些野生动物。听力文本从学生熟悉的环境出发，发掘珠海的环境资源，通过对学生身边的野生动物进行介绍，融教学与生活为一体——让英语走进生活，让生活走进英语课堂。

文本融合了前面学过的几个主题的知识点，包括通过野生动物的外貌特征、生活习惯和属性等因素以及它们的生活环境来描述动物。教师围绕该文本，引导同学们展开听说学习。不仅能锻炼学生的英语听力，还能调动他们的思维。听说训练过程中，从整体理解文本到分段理解文本，激发孩子思考。大量听力信息的输入，不断培养学生对选择性、细节性信息的听力技巧。分文段把听到的词语圈出来，然后对动物进行介绍。活动中学生对听力信息进行整理、概括和总结，提高了英语语言技能和综合能力。

六年级主题 4　Feelings

听力材料

It was the Christmas Eve yesterday. I decorated the Christmas tree with my sister. My mother was proud of us. My family members had a big dinner together. We were very happy . After dinner, we played the monopoly game. My sister and I lost the game. I was sad. And then we put big stockings on the chimney before sleeping.

It was the midnight when I heard the noise in my bedroom. 'Who's that?!' I was scared and worried. I got up and went to the living room. There were lots of presents under the Christmas tree. Suddenly, I was excited! Maybe the Santa Claus put them there. I looked around, but there was no one there. Wait! A Christmas hat was under my big stocking. Who left it here?

What an amazing night!

听说活动

1. T: Listen to the first paragraph and tell what the festival is about.

A
the Spring Festival

B
Christmas Eve

C
the Mid-autumn Festival

2. T: What can people do in this festival?

3. T: Let's listen to the whole passage and number the pictures.

( )

( )

( )

( )

( )

( )

4. T: Let's listen to the whole passage again and fill in the past tense words to the right places.

got	looked	had	heard	went
decorated	put	lost	was	played

1) I ________ the Christmas tree with my sister.

2) My family members __________ a big dinner together.

3) We ____ the monopoly game.

4) My sister and I ___ the game.

5) We ___ big stockings in the chimney before sleeping.

6) I _____ the noise in my bedroom.

7) I ___ up and ___ to the living room.

8) I _____around, but there ___ no one there.

5. T: Listen to the whole passage again and match the emotions with the right pictures.

6. T: Try to retell the story with your group members by using the pictures above.

7. T: Can you guess who left the Christmas hat there?

Please discuss with your group members, and give an ending to this story.

课程设计者：珠海市香洲区第一小学 曾辰赟

圣诞节在西方是一个重要节日，相当于我们中国的春节。中国学生也通过各种方式和渠道对圣诞节的活动有了许多了解。这个听力文本以圣诞节的前一天——平安夜为背景，介绍了欢乐温馨的圣诞活动，同时引出了惊喜有趣的半夜“抓圣诞老人”的小故事。故事编排合理，情节有趣，结尾留下悬念，引发学生浓厚的学习兴趣。

本创编文本综合了六年级上册的多个知识点，包括一般过去时、不规则动词过去式的运用，以及本单元表达情绪的形容词。教师在展开听说练习的过程中引导学生提取关键信息，渗透听读技巧，让学生有效地学习语言。通过对故事的深层次听读训练，吸引学生进入故事，体验故事人物的不同情感。

整个听读训练从提取信息过程中了解故事概况，到细节搜寻输出故事情节，再到整合图文口头复述，都为学生的逻辑推理提供了有效线索和铺垫，让学生通过基础知识的升华创作出自己的故事。学生的听说能力在不断的输入和触发中得到了很好的锻炼。

六年级主题 5 Famous People

听力材料

There are many famous people in China. They contributed a lot to our country.

Yuan Longping is a Chinese agricultural scientist. He was born in September, 1930 in Beijing. He was from Jiangxi. He loved playing the violin and swimming. Mr. Yuan cultivated the first hybrid rice varieties in the 1970s. He solved the problem of food in the world. And he won many prizes. He was called the "Father of Hybrid Rice".

Zhong Nanshan is one of the famous doctors and medical scientists. He was born in October, 1936 in Nanjing. He likes exercising very much. 17 years ago, Dr. Zhong saved lives and treated patients from SARS. In 2020, the 84–year–old doctor still fought against the coronavirus.

Su Bingtian is an Asian "flying man". He was born in 1989 in Zhongshan, Guangdong. He ran so fast in the men's 100–meter dash at the Tokyo Olympics. Su also became the first Asian runner to reach the Olympic final of the event.

In June, 2021, **Nie haisheng**, **Liu Boming** and **Tang Hongbo** went into the space by the Shenzhou XII. After three months, they finished their tasks and came back. It's successful.

All of these Chinese famous people are our heroes. We admire and love them so much.

听说活动

1. T: Listen to the first paragraph and the second paragraph. Guess who he is and tick "√".

Zhong Nanshan	Yuan Longping	Nie Haisheng Liu Boming Tang Hongbo
(　　)	(　　)	(　　)

2. T: Listen to the third paragraph. What do you know about him? Can you say some key words or sentences? Can you guess who will be talked about later?

3. T: Let's listen to the whole passage and Write the below number the names.

Su Bingtian	Nie Haisheng Liu Boming Tang Hongbo
(　　)	(　　)

Yuan Longping (　　　)	Zhong Nanshan (　　　)

4. T: Let's listen to the whole passage again and put the right number of the pictures in the blanks.

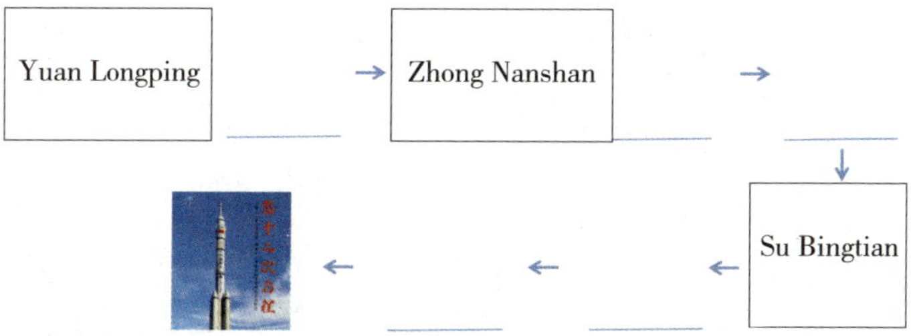

A

Nie Haisheng
Liu Boming
Tang Hongbo
B

C

Yuan Longping
D

Zhong Nanshan
E

5. T: Listen to the whole passage again, pick out the past tense words you heard and fill in the table.

Yuan Longping	Zhong Nanshan	Su Bingtian	Nie Haisheng, Liu Boming, Tang Hongbo
was, cultivated, ...			

教师给每个分好的小组发一个信封，装入一些不规则动词的过去式的单词，其中包含语篇中下划线的单词。每个组配有一个大表格任务单。学生将再次听完整个语篇，在听的过程中，小组内进行 Pick up the Words 的竞赛，把听到的不规则过去式拣出来，贴入表中相应的人物下方，学生根据表格中的人物和关键动词组织语言，每人用一两句话描述文中的著名人物，其他同学可不断补充，最终复述出整篇文章。

6. T: Listen and read the passage. Answer the questions.

- Who impress you most? Can you talk more about him?
- Can you tell us other famous Chinese people? Why?
- What can you do to make contribution to our country?

课程设计者：珠海市香洲区第一小学 黄颖

该听力文本介绍了中国的著名人物，袁隆平、钟南山、苏炳添、神舟十二号宇航员聂海胜、刘伯明和汤洪波。他们都是现在社会的热点话题人物。教材中侧重介绍的是历史上的著名人物，这篇听力文本作为拓展补充素材，用英文给学生介绍了当下的中国名人以及他们的事迹和贡献。这些人物学生都非常熟悉。在英语课堂中，教师通过递进式的丰富多样的任务和图片，使学生加深对这些文章的理解，降低了听说学习的难度，同时也激发了学生的学习热情和爱国情怀。

该听力文本的语言点主要是一般过去时的运用、不规则动词的过去式的巩固和情感态度的表达。以它为底本开展听说学习，突出学科语言和学科思维。任务单的题目设置和图片，可以让学生将视觉和听觉结合起来，进而提高听说能力。在听说训练过程中，首先分主题段落播放，让学生初步认识主题。接下来再让学生对听力全文进行细节把握，激发思维和推理能力。在听说活动中，学生需要不断听材料去完成图片排序、选词填表，复述文章等任务。活动设置主要是完整不间断的文本听力输入，可以让学生进行连续性的思考。其中，选词填表项让学生对文章进行归纳梳理，提高了学生对语篇内容的归纳能力。其后，通过小组讨论、互相交流等形式，鼓励学生根据表格信息进行有意义的表达，有效整合了语言知识和语言技能，提升了学生的思维概括能力，达到了以听促说的深度学习效果。

六年级主题6 The Spring Festival

听力材料

The Spring Festival is the most important festival in China. It's usually in January or February. Before that, Chinese people get together to celebrate the festival. There are many customs about the Spring Festival.

The Spring Festival is coming. Lily and her family are going to fly back to their hometown, Guangdong. On the first day, Lily is going to help her parents do some chores. Because the spring-cleaning is a traditional custom. It means to sweep away bad luck. On the second day, Lily's mother, Laura, is going to make sweet dumplings and Lily is going to learn to make them. Because it means reunion. On the third day, Lily's father, John, is going to shop for new clothes and couplets with his family. After shopping, they are going to paste spring poems on the door. Because the spring poems express their best wishes for the next year.

On the eve of the Spring Festival, Lily is going to visit her grandparents with her parents. They are going to get together and have a big dinner. They are going to sing and dance. At 12 o'clock at the midnight, people are going to set off fireworks to celebrate the new year. At this time, Lily's grandparents are going to give her red pockets. And the red pockets stands for good luck. Lily will be very happy.

On the Spring Festival, the family is going to watch the show of the dancing dragon and lion. How wonderful!

听说活动

1. T: Listen to the first paragraph and choose the best title for the passage.

A. The New Year　　B.The Spring Festival　　C.Winter Holiday

2. T: Why do you choose the answer? Can you say out the key words that you heard?

3. T: Listen to the whole passage and number the pictures about the plan of Lily's family.

(　　)

(　　)

(　　)

(　　)

(　　)

(　　)

(　　)

(　　)

(　　)

4. T: Listen for the third time, and find out the reasons of the customs, and then match them.

best wishes	good luck	sweep away bad luck	reunion

5. T: Group work: Four students forms a group, to talk about their hometown and the different customs about the Spring Festival, and then try to draw it out on the worksheet.

6. T: Supposing you are a cultural propaganda ambassador(文化宣传大使), can you introduce the Spring Festival to the foreigners?

课程设计者：珠海市香洲区第一小学 马志慧

春节是最重要的传统节日，学生对这个节日再熟悉不过了。本文以 Lily 一家的返乡计划为主线，配上与春节有关的活动插图，在英语课堂中，引导学生回想起自己过年前以及过年时家里的情景，激活学生头脑中的相关信息。

创编文本整合了本单元的重难点知识，包括一般将来时的表达和表示活动的动词词组的运用。以旧知识为切入点，在复习学过的词组时，拓展学生们在日常生活中比较了解的、但不会用英文表达的习俗词组。以一般将来时为底本的听说学习，突显英语学科的整合性和学科思维。本次听说训练把握到活动的难度，设计了阶梯进式的听说活动。首先，听部分内容选取文本主题，激发学生思考，锻炼学生的概括能力。同时，举证说明所选取答案的关键词，训练学生们的信息提取能力。接着，通过不间断的听说活动，整体感知材料，提升认知，激发学生的逻辑思维。

学生在整体感知文本信息后，发现自己家乡的春节习俗和本文所述的异同，画出并分享家乡过年的习俗，提升了学生的语言素养。最后，作为一名中国文化的宣传大使，向外国友人介绍春节的习俗，此环节整合了语言知识和语言技能，增强了学生的逻辑思维能力和概括能力。

六年级主题 7 Visiting Zhuhai

听力材料

My name is Ken. I was born in Zhuhai. It is a Special Economic Zone in the south of Guangdong. The name "Zhuhai" means Pearl River flowing into the South Sea.

The weather in Zhuhai is semi-tropical. There is not much difference in the temperature in a year. It is generally hot, and the average temperature is about 22.5°C. We always wear T-shirts and pants. It often rains from April to September. Is it cold in winter? Well, rare! It is cool and dry in winter. It hardly snows. Sweaters are enough for us. So, when is the best time to visit Zhuhai? Probably it is in autumn and winter.

There are rich cultural traditions in Zhuhai. For example, Zao Cha culture is well-known. People have dim sum in local teahouses to enjoy the morning for a while. Flower Arranging is a unique custom. When it is the Spring Festival, people buy flowers and pot plants to display in their houses.

There are also lots of celebrities in Zhuhai. Rong Guotuan was one of them. Nanping town, now part of Zhuhai, was his hometown. Rong was born in Hong Kong on August 10, 1937. His father was a seaman. Later, his family moved back to mainland China and in 1943, Rong went to Zhenxian School.

His hobby was playing ping-pong. When he was seven, he became the "King of Ping-Pong" in the school. When he was twenty-two, he won the men's singles at the 25th World Ping-Pong Championships and became China's first world champion.

听说活动

1. Listen and predict.

T: Listen to the first paragraph and find out the topic.

T: What aspects will it possibly talk about?

2. Listen and match.

T: Let's listen to the second paragraph and choose the correct graphs for the temperature and rainy days in Zhuhai.

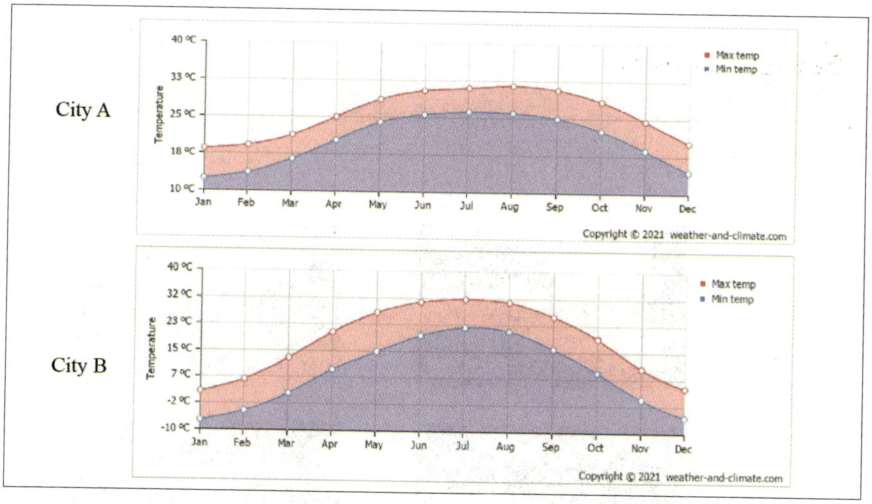

(Max and min temperature)

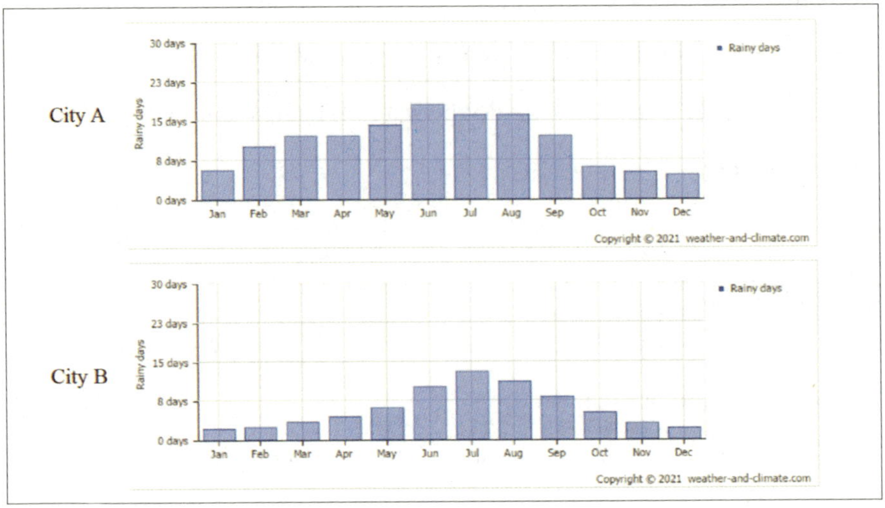

(Rainy days)

(1) Discussion about the weather in different seasons.

T: What's the weather like in spring/summer/autumn/winter? What clothes will you wear?

3. Listen and tick.

T: Listen to the third paragraph and tick the cultural traditions in Zhuhai.

(　　)

(　　)

(　　)

(　　)

(1) Discussion about cultural traditions.

T: How often do your family have Zao Cha? How many types of flowers or pot plants do your family usually buy? And what color are they?

T: What other traditions do you know?

4. Listen and order.

T: Let's listen to the last paragraph and put the events (right pictures) in the correct order with your partner.

老师提前将印有时间线的 A4 纸、事件条及 6 张图片放入信封，学生两人为一组，根据听到的内容按时间给事件条及图片排序，并尝试用简短的句子介绍容国团。

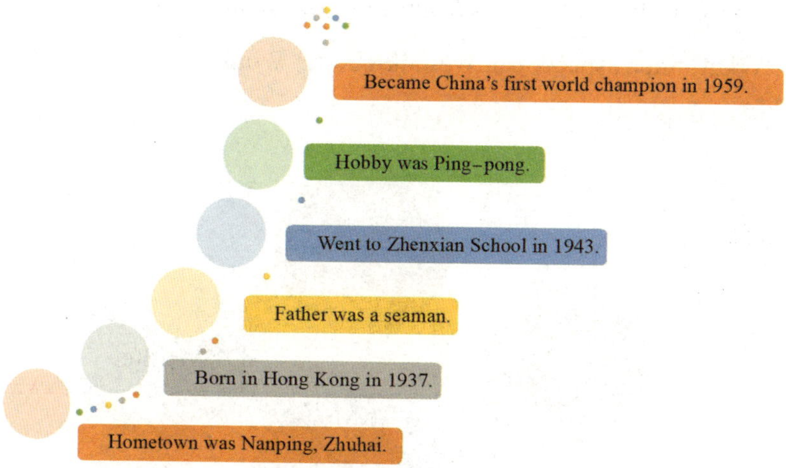

Rong Guotuan

Rong Guotuan	Rong Guotuan

(1) Discussion about personal information.

T: Where is your hometown? When were you born? What does your father/mother do? Where is your school? What is your hobby? Did you win a prize?

5. Listen and summarize.

T: Listen to the passage again and summarize the content into a mindmap.

T: What other aspects can we talk about? Would you like to share about them?

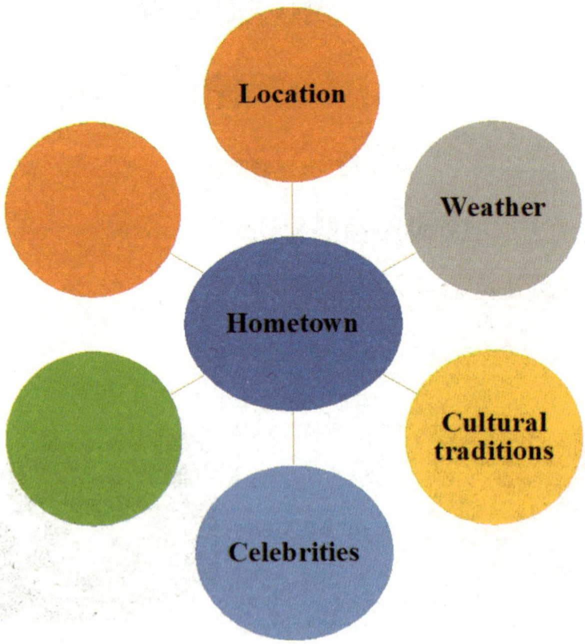

6. Discuss and introduce.

T: Where is your hometown? Think about it with the outline in your mind map and then share it with us.

课程设计者：珠海市香洲区第二小学 卿小仪

本单元旨在以多形式的语言活动帮助学生复习以前所学话题的重点词汇和功能句，引导学生综合运用所学知识和技能进行交流。创编文本通过本土化的材料，让语篇贴近学生的生活，并搭建任务阶梯，逐步丰富学生的英语表达能力，引导学生实现运用英语语言进行真正的文化交际与文化输出，实现深度学习的目的。

创编文本借由 Ken 出生于珠海引出语篇的主题——介绍家乡，先从地理位置和名字由来整体介绍，随后从气候（温度、降水）、人文（习俗、名人）两大方面细致介绍珠海。在逐步呈现听力文本的过程中，借助图片辅助理解，并通过拓展性问题复习巩固旧知，挖掘更多的文本内涵，引导学生进行深度联想，构建有意义的、有互动的对话，丰富学生的认知框架，以利于后续的表达与分享。

把听力输入的语言，制作成思维导图，并用作口头表达的范本，在这过程中，学生从模仿、归纳、拓展到再创，有效地架构语言认知，整合学习策略，提升了听说能力。

六年级主题 8 All Around Me

听力材料

A wise mother would try to find a good environment for her children's best education.

Mencius's mother is a great mother of Zou State. To make her son get a good education, she moved her house three times.

When Mencius was a child, he lived near a graveyard. Therefore, he often played near the grave and imitated people's crying or digging the tombs. When his mother saw this, she decided to move. She said: "The environment was not good for his son's education. It's not a good place for a child to live in."

Then they moved to a house near a market. Soon Mencius began to imitate people's hawking and bargaining. He found it interesting and played the game with his friends again and again. His mother found this place still not good for a child to live in. She decided to move away again.

At last, they settled down near a school and library. Before long, Mencius began imitating the students' reading and writing. He became more polite and hardworking. Then his mother said: this is a good place for a child to live in.

When Mencius grew up, he was well-known for his politeness and talent.

This story tells us a good educational environment is very important for children.

听说活动

1. T: Where did Mencius live when he was a child? What did he do there?
( )

2. T: Where did Mencius go for the second move? What did he do there?
( )

3. T: Where did Mencius go for the third move? What did he do there?
( )

A. A market. He began to imitate people's hawking and bargaining.

B. A graveyard. He played near the grave and imitated people's crying or digging the tombs.

C. A school and library. He began imitating the students' reading and writing.

上述三个问题答案的反复出现，让学生思考并区分每次搬家的地点和所做的事情，为后续的复述文本做铺垫。

1. T: Let's listen to the whole passage and number the pictures.

( )

( )

( )

（ ）

（ ）

2. For a student, which place of the following is the best place to live?

（ ）

A. Near Chinese restaurant and art gallery.

B. Near coffee shop and park.

C. Near public library and school.

课程设计者：珠海市横琴新区第一小学 毕群

本单元的学习内容是环境话题，该听力文本从学生学习主题、学生主体、学生发展、创新精神、活学活用等方面出发，整合改编了六年级学生较为熟悉的民间故事《孟母三迁》。以民间故事为听力文本，不单是传授知识，更多的是为学生的发展创造条件。创编文本把故事的地点词与课本学习的词语相融合，勾起学生对中文故事的回顾，激活学生的主体意识，激发学生浓厚的学习兴趣，引发学生的深度思考。

创编文本把中国文化渗透在英语听说学习中，学生通过已知的中文故事完成英语的听读练习。学生在听说过程中，听取细节、寻找线索，进行推理，语言知识学习和听说能力都能得到提高。

把听力输入的语言，用作口头看图说话或复述故事情节，学生需要一次次地进行思考、总结和表达，有效整合了语言知识和语言技能，提升了概括能力。

六年级主题 9　Daily Life

听力材料

There was a frog who made his home in a shallow well. One day he met a turtle from the East Sea.

"I'm so happy!" The frog told the turtle.

"When on the ground, I would jump up and down in the well. When I'm tired, I would go to sleep in the bed. Every day, I can do many things that I like. For example, I usually get up at 8:00, then I have breakfast at 8:30. It's a good habit for me. Sometimes, I eat sandwiches for breakfast. After breakfast, I often go swimming in the water. Back in the water, I would swim with only my head above the surface. You should come to visit me sometimes."

The turtle said, "I can't tell you how big the East Sea is. There are many different animals in it. We can play with toys every day. And there are all kinds of food and drinks we can choose from. That is amazing!"

On hearing the turtle, the frog was so surprised.

听说活动

1. T: Listen to the first paragraph and guess what the topic is about.

2. T: How do you know it is about them? What keywords did you hear?

3. T: Let's listen to the whole passage and number the pictures.

4. T: Let's listen to the whole passage again and put the right pictures in the blanks.

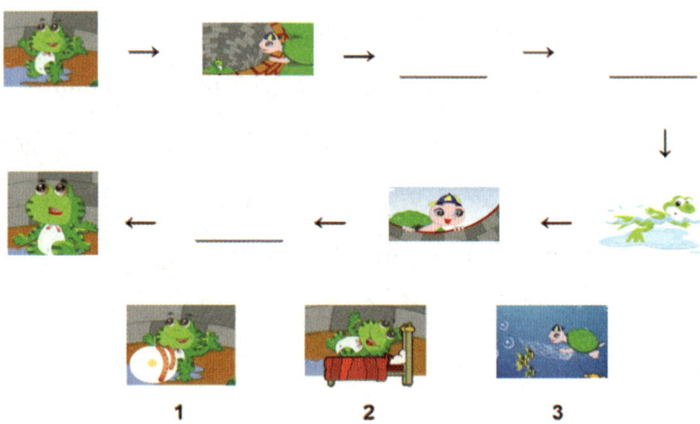

5. T: Listen to the whole passage again and pick out the past tense words you heard.

教师给每个分好的小组发一个信封，装入一些动词短语，其中包含语篇中下划线的单词。学生将再次听完整个语篇，在听的过程中，小组内进行 Pick up the Words 的竞赛，把听到的文本中的动词短语挑出来，看谁挑得多。这些动词短语就是听力文本的关键词，教师邀请学生把关键词贴在对应的图画上，学生根据图画的情节和关键词所搭建的脚手架，用自己的画简单地说出每个细节，最终串联起整个故事。

6. T: Listen, read and answer two questions.

- What happened next?
- Do you want to live with this frog in the well? Why?

课程设计者：珠海市香洲区第二小学 陈莉

《井底之蛙》是耳熟能详的寓言故事，富有趣味性和哲理性。该听力文本立足于中文故事脉络，结合本单元主题 *Daily Life*，在简化原文本故事的基础上又丰富了单元主题和知识要点。学生在熟悉的文本带动下，能更有兴趣、更加顺畅地掌握知识。

创编文本主要结合了青蛙的日常活动，融入本单元的生词如 sandwich, habit 等及进阶词语 shallow well, different, get up, go to sleep, have breakfast 等，

还涵盖了 There was ... / I ... at... 等句式。

文本围绕《井底之蛙》这个寓言故事进行深度学习和“听、说、读、写”的训练，在语境中呈现出了一般现在时的用法，通俗易懂，集知识性、娱乐性、趣味性于一体，增强了学生学习英语的兴趣。

六年级主题 10　Free Time

听力材料

There is a young man, Lord Ye. He likes dragons very much. In his free time, he often does many things. Every morning, he gets up early, then he goes to many clubs. In China, there are many other clubs, such as chess club, art club, and music club. Usually, he goes to these clubs, but not every week.

His favorite club is the art club because he has a hobby of painting. In his free time, He draws many dragons in his house. The house becomes a world of the dragon.

"We can draw dragons together, my friend." He always talks about dragons with others.

A real dragon hears of Lord Ye, and it is so happy. He wants to visit Lord Ye and makes a friend with him.

"Hi, Mr. Ye! Nice to meet you." The real dragon comes to visit, but Mr. Ye runs away as fast as he can. "Oh, my God! Help! Help!" He runs and shouts.

听说活动

1. T: Listen to the first paragraph and guess what the topic is about.

A. 
B. 
C. 

2. T: How do you know it is about them? What keywords did you hear?

3. T: Let's listen to the whole passage and number the pictures.

( )

( )

( )

( )

4. T: Let's listen to the whole passage again and choose the clubs you heard.

1

2

3

5. T: Listen to the whole passage again and pick out the past tense words you heard.

教师给每一个小组发一个信封，装入一些关于日常活动的动词、名词短语，其中包含语篇中下划线的短语。学生将再次听完整个语篇。在听的过程中，小组内进行 Pick up the Words 的竞赛，把听到的文本中的日常活动的动词、名词短语挑出来，看谁挑得多。这些日常活动的动词、名词短语就是听力文本的关键词，教师邀请学生把关键词贴在与之相对应的图画上，学生根据图画的情节和关键词所搭建的脚手架，用自己的画简单地说出每个细节，最终串联起整个故事。

6. T: Listen and read the story and answer Mom's questions.

- What is your favorite animal? Why?
- How do you feel about Mr. Ye's story?

课程设计者：珠海市香洲区第二小学　陈莉

《叶公好龙》是一篇耳熟能详的寓言故事，也蕴含了丰富的道理。通过传统文化的英语翻译表达，学生们能从原本熟悉的故事入手，进入英语的课堂学习中。学生在英语的语言环境和中文故事的脉络中，用有趣的传统故事，勾起浓厚的学习兴趣。

该文本，一是遵照了《叶公好龙》的传统中文脉络，二是结合单元主题“Free Time”和“Hobby”进行了整合改编，三是涵盖了部分较为进阶的单词如 dragon、together 等和固定短语 long long ago、on his free time、with others 等，四是结合了多单元的知识点，包括一般现在时的实际运用、动词以及名词短语的巩固和情感态度的表达。

本文围绕《叶公好龙》这个寓言故事进行深度学习和“听、说、读、写”的训练，在轻松活泼的英语知识点学习过程中，使学生们学到表里如一、言行一致等人生道理，实现用英语讲述经典寓言故事、传统文化和人生哲理的多重教学目的。

六年级主题 11 Nature and Culture

听力材料

The Chinese New Year is the most important festival for Chinese people. It's also called the Spring Festival. The date of the Chinese New Year changes every year. But it's usually **in January or February**. With the wishes for happiness and good luck, people **clean the houses**, **put up spring couplets (Chunlian in Chinese)** and **Fu** characters. On the eve of the Chinese New Year, people **have a big dinner** with their families. After dinner, they **watch the CCTV Spring Festival Gala**, **chat**, and **stay up late** to welcome the new year. Children are especially happy because they can **get lucky money** in red envelopes.

On the Chinese calendar, each year is represented by a **zodiac animal** (known as Shengxiao). There are twelve animals in a cycle. In order, they are Rat, Ox, Tiger, Rabbit, Dragon, Snake, Horse, Goat, Monkey, Rooster, Dog, and Pig. 2021 is the year of Ox. What about 2022? Do you know the answer?

听说活动

1. T: Guess what festival it is according to the sentences.

(1) It's a Chinese traditional festival.

(2) People have a big dinner together.

(3) People wear new clothes.

(4) It's in winter.

2. T: What do you know about the Spring Festival? Please talk about it in one sentence.

3. T: Listen to the whole passage again and tick the subjects you heard about the Spring Festival.

( ) the story of Nian ( ) the date

( ) the celebration ( ) the zodiac animals

( ) the weather ( ) Chinese New Year songs

4. T: Listen to the first paragraph and number the pictures.

( )

( )

( )

( )

( )

( )

5. T: Listen to the second paragraph and complete the order of animals in the Chinese zodiac.

Rat → Ox → _______ → _______ →Dragon → _______

→ Horse→ Goat→ _______ → Rooster → _______ → _______.

6. T: Listen to the whole passage again and pay attention to the details you missed.

7. T: Do you know more about the Spring Festival after these listening activities? What do you know? Please tell us.

8. T: What's your favorite festival? When is it? How do to celebrate it? Please talk about your favorite festival and share it in groups.

课程设计者：珠海市香洲区湾仔小学　郭思英

本单元的主题为自然与文化，涉及天气、节日、动物等话题。因此，创编文本以春节为主题，介绍春节的习俗及生肖，情境贴近学生生活，能引起学生共鸣，帮他们树立文化自信。

在听前阶段，教师采用猜谜的方式引出主题，然后让学生进行头脑风暴，说说他们所了解的春节。目的在于激活学生的背景知识，引导他们预测听力文本内容，提高听力效果，训练听前预测和联想的策略。在听中阶段，学生听一遍全文，验证他们的预测，获取主旨信息；然后再听文本的第一段及第二段，给图片编号及填写十二生肖，学习捕捉关键词，获取细节信息，锻炼记笔记、意象等听力认知策略。接下来，学生再完整地听一遍全文，查找之前没能听懂的语言点，自我评价前两遍听力中所使用策略的效果。在听后活动中，教师让学生说一说增加了哪些对春节的了解，锻炼学生的语言能力和思维以及归纳总结能力。最后学生讨论分享自己最喜欢的节日，借鉴听力文本进行知识迁移。通过整个听说课程，学生在参与、思考、运用、迁移中达到深度学习的目的。

六年级主题 12 Summer Vacation

听力材料

Dear Jenny,

Last summer vacation, I went to Guangzhou. It's the capital city of Guangdong Province. I went there by plane. I climbed the Baiyun Mountain in the morning. In the afternoon, I visited the Guangzhou Tower. And I enjoyed the view along the Pearl River on an evening cruise. You can't miss it when you visit Guangzhou. The city is famous for its food. I went to a restaurant for Canton morning tea, ate lots of delicious dim sum, and drank tea. It's so relaxing. I ate Tingzai porridge and wonton noodles, too. I stayed in Guangzhou for three days and had a good time.

There is another famous city in Guangdong. It's Zhuhai. I am going there next summer vacation by train. I'm going to stay there for two days. I want to visit the Chimelong Ocean Kingdom and the Zhuhai Opera House. I am going to Wailingding Island and play on the beach. I want to eat some seafood, too. I can't wait! I can send you a postcard from Zhuhai at that time.

Write soon,

Lily

听说活动

1. T: Listen to a letter and answer the questions.

(1) Who wrote the letter?

(2) Where did she go last summer vacation?

(3) Where is she going next summer vacation?

2. T: Listen to the first paragraph and number the pictures.

(　　)

(　　)

(　　)

(　　)

(　　)

(　　)

3. T: Listen to the second paragraph and complete the travel plan.

Travel Plan	
City	
Transportation	
Time to stay	
Places to visit	Chimelong Ocean Kingdom ________________ Wailingding ________
Food to eat	

4. T: Listen to the whole passage and pay attention to the details you missed.

5. T: Retell the passage according to the chart. If it's difficult for you, you can start with one paragraph.

	Last Summer Vacation	Next Summer Vacation
City	Guangzhou	Zhuhai
Transportation	plane	train
Time to stay	three days	two days
Places to visit	Baiyun Mountain Guangzhou Tower Pearl River	Chimelong Ocean Kingdom Zhuhai Opera House Wailingding Island
Food	dim sum/ tea Tingzai porridge wonton noodles	seafood

6. T: Let's talk about your last summer vacation and the travel plan for this summer vacation in groups. The following questions are some tips for you.

(1) Where did you go last summer vacation?

How did you get there?

What is it famous for?

What did you do there?

(2) Where are you going next summer vacation?

What are you going to do there?

课程设计者：珠海市香洲区湾仔小学　郭思英

本单元的主题为假期出行，涉及交通、服饰、食物、计划等话题。在本单元中，学生学习了如何综合运用一般现在时、一般过去时和一般将来时及相关旅游词汇来介绍自己的旅游情况。基于此，该听力创编文本以Lily的暑假为主题，介绍广州及珠海的著名景点及美食，让学生在本节听说课程中收获语言知识和技能，同时积累人文知识，提高人文素养。

教师通过让学生听第一遍文章并回答三个提纲性问题，引导学生获取基础信息，对文章有初步的了解。然后，再分别听第一段及第二段，完成给图片编号及填写假期计划的任务，引导学生捕捉关键词，获取细节信息，训练学生运用记笔记、意象等听力认知策略。接下来，让学生再完整地听一遍全文，引导学生关注之前错过或未能理解的关键点，为之后的语言输出做铺垫。在听后活动中，首先通过表格复述，引导学生进行自我评价和反思，评估自身是否掌握了目标语言。然后学生以同伴分享的形式，说说自己的暑假，实现知识的迁移与创造，培养运用语言的能力。通过一系列具有挑战性和引领性的学习任务，学生将掌握基础知识及听力策略，综合运用知识，达到深度学习的目的。